THE SONG OF SANO TAROT

THE SONG OF SANO TAROT

The Seven Forces of Creation

ANNA FULLWOOD

Radiant Books
New York

The Song of Sano Tarot was originally published under the pen name Nancy Fullwood in 1929. Illustrated by Vinegarice.

Illustrations © 2023 by Radiant Books

Library of Congress Control Number: 2023950654

Published in 2023 by Radiant Books
radiantbooks.co

ISBN 978-1-63994-048-6 (hardback)
ISBN 978-1-63994-049-3 (paperback)
ISBN 978-1-63994-050-9 (e-book)

CONTENTS

Foreword . . . . *ix*
Author's Introduction . . . . *xiii*

The Song of Sano Tarot

Prefatory 3

Book One
The Seven Songs of Tarot

1. The Royal Road to Peace Through the Vibratory Law of the Universe. 7
2. The Sexes on the Royal Road to Peace. 21
3. The Royal Road to Peace Through Service of the Race . 24
4. The Timekeeper on the Royal Road to Peace 30
5. The Forces on the Road to Peace 37
6. Joining the Forces on the Royal Road to Peace 40
7. The Joining of the Sexes on the Royal Road to Peace on the Planet Earth 47

Book Two
The Song of the Timekeeper

The People's Hope of Happiness in the Realm of Earth. . . 53

Book Three
Reproduction as the Gods Would Have It

Preface 85
Reproduction as the Gods Would Have It 87

Book Four
Hermitage Songs

The Song of Moses................................. 101
The Song of Timothy 106
The Song of Samuel................................ 115
The Song of Judith................................. 121
The Song of Israel.................................. 132
The Song of the King's Harpist 139
The Song of the Magician........................... 142
The Song of Michael 146

> "And they sing a new song."
> — *Revelation 5:9*

FOREWORD

This is an amazing book in the exact meaning of the word, which is "to overwhelm with wonder." It will not have that effect on all readers; to some, it may seem merely childish, because it is childlike — a very different matter. It appears to be addressed to "the children of this generation, wiser than the children of light" — wiser, that is, than those who judge everything by the hard, cold light of the purely rational intelligence.

When I say that this is an amazing book, I do not refer to the manner in which it came into being, or to the seemingly miraculous circumstances attendant upon that precipitation. These things I prefer to ignore, because they are as prejudicial to one type of mind as they are persuasive to another. It is as easy to make claims to supernatural inspiration as it is difficult to justify them. Therefore the only test of the validity of such claims lies — and should lie — in the very texture of the thing itself: Does it belong to the timeless, the archetypal world, or is it only another shadow in a world of shadows? All other criteria avail nothing. That this book stands such a test is my belief, arrived at both by intuition and by reason. Intuition is so personal a thing that however compelling it may be to oneself it can never be explained or justified to another; for a reasoned conclusion, however, one should be able to give reasons, and here are mine.

Like many another mariner shipwrecked on this shoal of time, I have always been on the lookout for rescuing sails on the metaphysical horizon — that is, for some resolving and revelatory teaching which should make possible the practical realization of one's spiritual life, the sense of which is no less sure and abiding than the sense of one's physical ephemerality and impotence. I found what I was looking for in the ancient wisdom of the East, a philosophy, a science, and a method suited to my needs. But this appears to be efficacious only for those who, like myself, are already deeply tinctured by some Oriental dye which makes them easily take the soul-color of the East. For others, differently constituted, something different is required, and in the course of time there gradually grew up in me a sense of what that something must be "like" — the elements it must contain and the conditions it must fulfill in order to meet the needs of the modern world.

I decided that such a teaching must be so simple that quite ordinary and untutored minds should be able to understand it, and yet so subtle that the most educated and extraordinary minds would not be able to comprehend it all. While it should throw new light upon the nature and constitution of the cosmos, even so it must concern itself with conduct — it must be both a theory and a method, in other words. But the one sure sign by which I fancied I should recognize this teaching would be that it should have something illuminating to say on the subject of sex, either actually or by implication.

The conditions which now govern the relations between men and women in the great centers of Anglo-Saxon civilization are in a true sense unprecedented by reason of the altered status of woman. Her so-called emancipation, and her invasion of fields hitherto pre-empted by man, has brought about, in countless cases, a reversal of metaphysical function, and this is the fertile cause of psychic and physical strains in both sexes which manifest themselves as abnormalities. Novels, plays, and tales are simply saturated with sex — everything, in point of fact, from society dancing to psycho-analysis.

Now these things indicate an acute intention of consciousness upon the relation between men and women in all its aspects, and portend profound changes in that relation, which, as it now exists, is the fertile cause of so much emotional misery and physical distress, quite aside from the dark shadow which it casts upon the future of humanity. Any teaching purporting to contain a new revelation would, therefore, of necessity (I argued) lay some kind of a healing hand upon this particular sore.

The Song of Sano Tarot meets all of the above-outlined conditions to some extent, and notably the last, for it is a book about sex in its cosmic aspect, which includes the microcosmic or human. Or, in deference to those who would claim that sex has no cosmic aspect, let me say rather that it is a book about the universal bipolar force, the positive aspect of which is represented on the plane human by man and the negative aspect by woman.

Because this book meets these conditions, I would not have it supposed that I regard it as a sacred scripture, like the Bhagavad Gita, the Dhammapada, or the New Testament. It lacks the pregnancy of phrase, the sublimity of expression, the spiritual "richness" of the true bibles of mankind, but it is in their dimension, nevertheless. What I do claim is that it is one of a small but increasing number of books now making their appearance, all dissimilar, but alike in this, that they point a way out of the slough of despond into which a materialistic science plunged us, books which envisage an animistic, rather than a mechanistic universe.

Science now points in this direction too, by its annihilation of its old conception of matter. For the newest science sees forms as only the interplay of forces; it sees these forces governed by mathematical law of such universality, beauty, and perfection as to imply the operation of a supernal intelligence, thus opening the door to the idea that forces are beings and that in phenomenality we witness the evidences of their activity; also, that beings, no less, are forces, powerful to the extent of their beingness, and that we ourselves, by reason of our beingness, can, through "the marriage of the Forces," become masters of life instead of being eternally doomed to be its slaves.

Here is glad news for mortals; here are glimpses which should make us less forlorn! This is a book which should be read without prejudice or preconception; not everyone can or will accept it, but those who are able cannot but be benefited, cannot but be blessed.

Claude Bragdon
Author of *Yoga for You*

AUTHOR'S INTRODUCTION
(1933)

Four years have passed since the first edition of *The Song of Sano Tarot* was published and delivered to its subscribers. During this time, it has traveled far and made many friends. Its fundamental truth and rhythm have acted like a spiritual leaven in the consciousness of many people, deepening their understanding of life and its law and widening their spiritual vision. It has made them aware that they are spiritual beings and that they can find equilibrium right here in the midst of the outer, chaotic, manmade world. The keynote of the book is *Balance* — the balance of the spiritual and physical natures, and according to the degree of balance attained, does intuition, which is the voice of the spirit, operate clearly.

My own understanding of what I have set down purely inspirationally has expanded greatly though I know that the work is as big and far-reaching as life itself and that my comprehension of it will continue to widen as I find my balance and live from my center of gravity rather than from the mental side of me. The intellect must take its place as the servant of the spirit. In its right place, it will expand and flower as it never could in its false, egotistical, self-assumed position as the mighty ruler of man.

Over a long period of years, I have had recurrences of extreme sensitiveness when my experiences are called *supernormal*, although they seem perfectly normal to me, and I am inclined to smile at having them called anything else. It was not my intention to write of these things. I feel that they are not important to anyone but myself, but a good and wise friend told me that the people who are interested in my writings have a legitimate curiosity to know something of their beginning and development. Perhaps my friend is right, so I am writing a new introduction to this third edition of *The Song of Sano Tarot*, in which I will touch upon the experiences which preceded the writing of this book, *The Tower of Light* and *The Life of One Woman*.

In these periods of which I have spoken, I am exceedingly clairvoyant. Nothing seems to be hidden from me. I think of friends, and immediately I am with them and see what they are doing. Something like a searchlight goes out from the middle of my body, and everything I turn this light upon is plainly visible. Friends have reported seeing me when I called on them in this *invisible* way. They minutely describe the clothes I have on, leaving no doubt that they see me, although my body is many miles away. I walk along strange streets and look in strange faces, and sometimes I hear bands playing and sometimes I hear beautiful singing. I have many songs I learned from invisible singers. There seems to be two of me, one sitting quietly watching the other one fare forth on adventure bent.

After one prolonged period of this kind I found that I was very nervous, so I stopped it voluntarily, although some of my friends said it was "blasphemous to give up such a gift." But I deliberately shut it out. I was living in Atlanta, Georgia, then and afterward we moved to Birmingham, Alabama. We lived in the country in beautiful Shades Valley, and I was much alone. I lived a wholesome out-of-door life raising boys and chickens, and my health was entirely restored.

For five years, I had no return of this phase of phenomena. Then right out of the blue, I had two amazing experiences. One night I was awakened by a terrific wind. I sat up in bed and literally had to hold the cover about me to keep it from being blown from the bed. At last, I got up and staggered in the wind to close the open window on the other side of the room, but when I raised my arms to lower the sash, I realized that there was no wind. It was a calm, full-moon night. Not a breath of air stirring. I could almost hear the trees breathing. Then later the same summer, I was awakened by fire. I sat up in bed wide awake, and the whole room was in a glow. It was light enough to have read by if I had had something to read, and all around the walls just below the picture molding were little tongues of flame. They were about a foot apart and might have been painted there like a border, except that they were alive and leaping, and on the wall to my left was a great bow knot of fire, throbbing like living coals. There are no words which can describe the stillness about me. I seemed to be in a vacuum where there was no living thing except the fire and me.

I sat there for what seemed ages until it all faded out. Then I went all over the house; the impression of fire was so strong. I knew nothing of symbolism, so could not interpret the experiences, but I met a man who was a student of these things, and he told me that accounts of symbolic visions had come down through the ages with certain results following them, so they had come to have definite meanings. He said the wind meant a revelation, that I was going to have something revealed to me. The tongues of flame, he said, meant the coming of a child or a new birth (in my case, a cosmic birth), and the bow knot of fire meant a religious upheaval.

This was about twenty years ago in the woods of Alabama, and there was no sign of great upheaval on any plane in my world. But today, we know that there has been a new birth in the world. Everything is changing. Even the man on the street today knows that something has happened to the world as we have known it, and that everything is in a state of upheaval. My friend said that it was his opinion that the wind was all in my own body, that every atom in it was being quickened, tuned up, as it were, preparatory to some greater phenomena, and that I had interpreted it as wind. I rather liked that idea, and in the light of what has happened since, I feel that it is true.

Five years passed again with no phenomenal experiences in my life. Then in the summer of 1917, I began to write. It was another extremely sensitive period. I kept hearing with an interior hearing and writing a strange word. At times it seemed to come from within myself; then again, it seemed from some far-off place. It had a ring and resonance, which always attracted my attention. The word was *Sano Tarot*. It was pronounced with the final "t" silent — "Tah-ro." Knowing nothing of the ancient doctrine of equilibrium called the *Tarot*, the word had no significance to me. Many impressions entirely new to me came in my mind. At first, the writing was more or less confused with my habits of thought and association of ideas. It seemed as if a very real person was speaking to me. I was frequently told to "clear the echo," which I learned meant to get my personal self out of the way. Sometimes I attempted to clothe the ideas with my own words, and I was cautioned thus: "Watch your mind action. You are intercepting, and I cannot speak."

What I wrote was far removed from anything I had ever known or heard of. I knew nothing of occultism, mysticism, or any sort of theory regarding life and its mysteries, and I didn't know one person who knew any more than I did about the things I wrote of. I came of generations of Scottish Presbyterian ministers. My paternal grandfather was a Presbyterian minister, and there were several ministers of this faith in my family. Someone has said that this was a perfect environment for my "super normal" experiences, for the Scots are a mystical, "canny" people. "Fey," some call them, and although I was never a particularly religious person, yet this devotional, mystical quality was in my blood, and may account, at least in part, for a sensitive side of me to which I had never given a name, having no terminology regarding such things.

I might as well have been recording a Sanskrit document, as far as my understanding of it went. But intuitively, I was swept on and on by its rhythm and truth. For I knew it was concrete, practical truth which was being taught to me, even though it seemed abstract and beyond my comprehension. As I obeyed the instruction given to me regarding the development of my "channel of intuition," there was less and less confusion. My contact with this higher dimension which Sano Tarot calls the *realm of Inspiration*, is always accompanied by great ecstasy, not only within myself but which communicates itself to those who are with me. Sano Tarot wields a strange and beautiful magic which dissolves our mundane illusions and lifts our consciousness into its own harmony and clear vision.

As I progressed with the recording, I learned that man lives in seven worlds, all of them operating in his own body, and that the prime reason for his being is to expand and polarize these worlds within himself so that he may have dominion over his own universe.

AUTHOR'S INTRODUCTION

In the summer of 1917, the "echo" was very clear, and I literally went to school in a new world under a group of teachers I couldn't see with material vision. They spoke of the center from which they operate as the "Hermitage, where the life Forces center, and from which they radiate to the far corners of the universe, which is the temple not made with hands." It is strange according to our human understanding, but it is very beautiful, harmonious, and true.

When the book was finished, I asked: "What must I do with it?"

The answer was: "The matter is in my hands. Make no move until I say move. I am preparing the minds of my people to receive my words. My people are waking from the sleep of material coma almost *en masse*.[1] Peace be with you."

So I waited ten years before the order came to move. Ten years packed with experience with its pleasures and its agonies.

I asked if it would not be well to condense the work, leaving out the many repetitions. The reply was: "Leave the work as you have recorded it. Rhythmic repetition is my method of expanding and building the brain cell of the people that they may more readily grasp the truth of my words."

In the year 1919, I received the order to "journey to New York." I was told to be in this city on my birthday, June 29th. Prevailing conditions made this apparently impossible, but quite without effort on my part, everything arranged itself. A change in my husband's business brought us to New York, and I have made my home here ever since. In New York, I had access to books and did much research work. I discovered that the essence of what I had written down was as old as the world. I found fragments of it in age-old documents and in ancient symbols. It has changed its form of presentation through the ages according to the need and interpretation of man, but the basic law of balance is the law of creation yesterday, today, and forever. I have found it in modern science clothed in erudite terminology. It is as modern as it is ancient and as practical as it is transcendental. The knowledge and use of it bring order into the chaos of our unbalanced Forces, which

---
[1] *En masse (French)* — as a whole; all together as a group.

in itself heals our wounds and clears our vision. The Timekeeper says: "Man's great work is himself. His place of operation is wherever he finds himself and his tools are the means at hand."

The law of balance shows us the truth of this statement and brings us back to basic principles and harmony.

I am learning to realize life in terms of Forces rather than form. The word *sex*, as Sano Tarot uses it, means much more than just the physical union of men and women. Every relationship on every plane is a marriage of Forces, either harmonious or discordant with its attendant results. What we call the *psychological moment*, when the universe seems to be working in harmony with our efforts, may be taken as an example of the balance of positive and negative Forces. If all parties to a proposition are positive, repulsion is the result, but if the positive and negative Forces represented balance each other, their fusion takes place, and something is conceived in harmony, which comes forth into material manifestation.

I asked Sano Tarot why the word *sex* was used throughout all the realms of vibratory movement, knowing its usual limited interpretation. The reply was: "It is the part of wisdom to expand a truth from its base. A word has no power to limit itself. A static interpretation of a word is the result of the limited consciousness of man. The people become blinded by their own immensity. As their consciousness expands, they are prone to give this expansion a new name, thus breaking the unity of vibration and confusing their own understanding of the Law. To the people, the word *sex* implies union; therefore, we work from this premise, carrying this basic truth to the far reaches of its expansion. The great pendulum of life swings far beyond the conception of material man and every stage of its movement is under one Law. Light will flood the minds of many people as they read my words. Give no troubled thought to this matter. The work is moving under my direction, and I say to you that all is well." — *Sano Tarot*.

The word *Tarot* is a symbol and means the Law — the unalterable cosmic Law of balance. Sano Tarot is also a symbol and means the law of the soul, the spiritual body balanced with its physical manifestation. The polarization or harmonious union of the opposite poles of the life Forces is the law of creation from the atom to man and superman, and life in all its many creative expressions is a great marriage song.

The whole message is given in terms of music, the vibratory humming of the life Forces. Every atom of our being is singing its own song. We are really great orchestras whose keynote sounds in the middle of our body. According to our realization of this truth and our ability to hold our keynote, does the orchestra give forth tones of beauty, which transmutes the discords into its own harmonious music.

I am a very practical person. Abstract theories do not interest me. I like things that "work," and after four years of observing the constructive, uplifting, and regenerative power of this spiritual Force operating under the symbol, Sano Tarot, I can truly say that it works.

The nature of my clairvoyant experiences has changed since that sensitive period of years ago. Sometimes I am among beings of enormous size and great beauty. I have been in the Sun and learned that it is not hot there, and I have been in the middle of the Earth and discovered another Sun there, which I have since been told is not a Sun, but is the "center of psychic energy." I have been in monasteries in faraway places, one of which I have written of in *The Tower of Light*. I have received information of which I cannot speak and many prophecies which have already come true and many yet to come. I presume that this will sound weird to many readers, though I am sure that others have had like experiences. To me, it is not at all weird. It is as natural as breathing to me. I wish to say here that it is my belief that some illumined scientist will discover that the Sun is much closer to Earth than the scientific measurements at present indicate. Perhaps we are actually in the Sun. The secret will be disclosed through the study of man himself, for man is the microcosm of the universe.

It is increasingly astonishing to me that this fundamental exposition of the law of balance was to appear in simpler form than I have found it elsewhere, through my hand. When the message is read with intuitive feeling, its effect is quite magical.

The law of balance has been called the *key to all mysteries*, and in this interpretation of it, the plan of universe building is laid on the table, and the gods, who have assisted in the polarization of the life Forces, though unseen, expound to the student the alchemical scheme of creation.

Anna Fullwood

THE SONG OF SANO TAROT

PREFATORY

Hear me, Sano Tarot:

In the minds of the people, light is now dawning, and in tones of sweetest music, they are vibrating on planes higher than ever before. The more sensitive of them are feeling that the old order of living is passing away. This is without doubt true, and this document on the law of vibratory polarization will more fully arouse their thought force and lift them into rarer realms of expression, where their vision will be clearer and their understanding more perfect.

In *The Seven Songs of Tarot*, many will find the whole vibratory law of life, and in *The Song of the Timekeeper*, others will see clearly what seemed obscure in *The Seven Songs*, and in *Reproduction as the Gods Would Have It*, the law of the right mating of the right vibrations is laid so bare that he who cares nothing of how life works in its great laboratory, Earth, must needs be impressed with the logic therein.

Many people will question as to the name God being used as though there were many gods. This has long been a source of misunderstanding among the people. As a matter of fact, I declare with them the same truth. We differ only in name. The word *god* in the ancient cipher code of vibration means a ruler or creative and motivating center of a given expression of the life Forces. The primal gods are seven in number. They have been likened to the seven spirits before the throne. Each is concerned only with the expansion and polarization of its own creation. These creations are the seven great primal Forces which cross themselves in the lowered vibratory realm of Earth, seeking balance one with the other, thus bringing the kingdom of harmony into Earth.

When the people read this story of creation told in terms of natural Forces, they will wonder from whence it came, for most truly, the recorder knew nothing of the vital chemical Forces in the great laboratory where the gods are working for the perfection of their kingdoms. The material expressions of life which seem so ultimate are the results of vibratory matings of degrees of the seven primal Forces. When the Forces fused are harmonious, expansion and growth follow, but separation and disintegration result from the fusion of inharmonious forces.

I beseech you to believe me when I say that dwelling on phenomena is of no moment. When you have balanced your physical and spiritual Forces, things hidden from you will be revealed, and you will know that you yourself are the veil which clouds your understanding.

You see — you people to whom I am speaking — that in this exposition of how life expands in the realm of Earth, the law of harmony not only makes new growth possible, but it is the only law whereby life can continue in material expression. So gain a real and comprehensive knowledge of the law of vibration.

The cycle of the expression of the spiritual Force Inspiration is now dawning. During its reign, many people will become conscious of the guidance of the gods through their channel of intuition, which will be perfected by the balancing of their spiritual and physical Forces. Then they will comprehend the truth of my words, and will demand that harmony sing in all their expressions of life. Know you this: Harmony is nature's first law and is the foundation of life's working plan. Where harmony is not, no good thing can be. Verily I, Sano Tarot who am the ruler of the great primal Force Inspiration, say this which is truth.

Where harmony is not, disintegration begins its deadly work, and ere much time is spent, most truly will death ensue. Now death has no part in life's perfect plan and comes only from breaking the law of balance in the fusion of the life Forces. I beseech you people who will read my words to give them deep intuitive thought, for herein I have given to you the secret of everlasting life and the solution of all the problems which vex you.

I leave the Book in your hands and the peace which passes understanding in your hearts.

I, Sano Tarot, have spoken.

Book One

THE SEVEN SONGS OF TAROT

1. THE ROYAL ROAD TO PEACE THROUGH THE VIBRATORY LAW OF THE UNIVERSE

Hear me, Sano Tarot:
 I speak to the people from the Hermitage, where the life Forces center and from which they radiate to the far corners of the universe, which is the temple not made with hands. Make ready to receive the truth of the gods!

Sano Tarot is the symbol under which the great primal Force Inspiration is now coming into full expression in the realm of Earth. Its vibratory music sings a high sweet song, and not every ear is attuned to its humming. I beseech you, my people, to lift your spirit high and listen in the still places for my song, whose keynote is Harmony and whose theme is balanced Forces.

Children of Earth, I hold you very dear.

I, Sano Tarot, who govern the fourth or Inspirational realm of being, have spoken.

The word *Tarot* may be interpreted as a royal road. There are seven royal roads to the still place where the life Forces make music of balance and sing of the peace which passes understanding. On each road, there are seven milestones which guide the seeker after truth. These milestones show the way to peace through the law of vibration, which is the law of life.

The seven royal roads are the seven realms of being, or the seven great primal Forces which govern life. The seven milestones are the seven degrees of vibration which form the complete expression of each realm of being, and these degrees of vibration, mated in their own realms, make the harmony of the spheres. The right Forces mated on the right degrees of their vibration sing through the universe in perfect accord, issuing tones of wondrous beauty.

I, Sano Tarot, have spoken.

The seven realms of being are the seven vibratory laws or Tarots of the universe.

Pano Tarot vibrates through the universe as pure Spiritual Mind.

Fano Tarot vibrations make the Force of Heart in the universe.

Tano Tarot vibrates the Force of Material Wealth in the universe.

Sano Tarot vibration makes the Force of Inspiration in the universe.

Rano Tarot vibrates the Force of Faith in the universe.

Gano Tarot vibrates the Force of Universal Love in the universe.

Ono Taro vibrates the Force of Hope in the universe.

These are the seven Tarots through which the gods lead the seeker after truth.

I, Sano Tarot, have spoken.

The primal Forces expand in the realm of Earth under cyclic law. Each Force lifts its tone above all others during the cycle of its reign. My Force, Inspiration, has sounded its note, and my cycle of expression has begun. Even now, the song of Tano Tarot is losing itself in my high music. I call my people out of the shadows of illusion into the sunlight of truth!

The road to peace is long and steep and fraught with danger to those who do not know the way. The seven vibratory laws of the universe each vibrate the song of the universe in its own realm. The songs of the universe sung in harmony are the right royal inspiration of the Seers on the spiritual heights of being.

The Seers are the people of Earth who have overcome the flesh as expressed on the lower planes of life and now serve on the three higher planes with no thought of self. The three higher planes of life's expression are Inspiration, Faith, and Universal Love. Overcoming the flesh is the highest test of the disciple on the road to peace.

I, Sano Tarot, say this, which is truth.

Vibrating on the right degrees of expression mates the Forces right royally in their own realms and issues the song of harmony.

Vibrating on the wrong degrees of expression makes songs of discord and death. Songs sung by the right Forces in their own realms of expression ring the bell of happiness and unite the spiritual Forces with the physical.

Hear me, Sano Tarot:
    I say that the time is ripe for the Seers of Earth to teach the truth of the gods to the people who express in their own realms of being. Riches of Earth and spiritual inheritance are for those who have sung the song of balanced Forces.
    I, Sano Tarot, say this, which is truth.

The song of balanced Forces is the song of the universe. The song of the universe is the singing of the right Forces in their own realms. The singing of the right Forces in their own realms on their own planes of development is the right royal mating of the physical Forces with the spiritual Forces. From the mating of the physical and spiritual Forces issues the harmony of the spheres. Sing to the right mating of the Forces on their own planes, and you will inspire the Great Gano Tarot, which is the Force of Universal Love.

Hear me, Sano Tarot:
    I say that the seven primal Forces sing to the right mates. Singing to the wrong mate brings destruction. Singing to the right singing mate on the right degree of expression sings of joy.
    The Force of Pano Tarot, which is the Force of Spiritual Mind, must sing to the Force of Pano Tarot or disintegrate.
    Singers of Fano Tarot, which is the Force of Heart, must attune their songs to Fano Tarot.
    Songs sung by Tano Tarot, which is the Force of Material Wealth, must join their songs to Tano Tarot.
    Inspiration sings to Sano Tarot, and the right royal answering song must be of Inspiration.
    The Force of Rano Tarot, which sings of Faith, sings back to the song of its own realm.

The Gano Tarot Force sings to the spirit of Universal Love, and its song returns the right royal vibration of itself.

Ono Tarot sings to itself of Hope, and all the universe responds to its song.

Sing the song of perfect mates! Inspire the right royal opening of the gates of Tarot!

I, Sano Tarot, have spoken.

Singing to the wrong mate sings of the overcoming of life by death. Hope will be destroyed, and utter desolation reign. Singers to the wrong mates in the wrong realms of being have cursed the planet Earth since the day when the King drove the rebellious Forces from the state of upheaval in the realm of Venus.[2]

The songs sung by the wrong mates have caused the Earth to sing songs of sorrow. The songs of sorrow have caused the death song of the people singing them.

Hear me: I, Sano Tarot, say that the right royal mates singing in their own realms make songs of harmony unspeakable.

---

[2] The realm of Venus may be more clearly comprehended if the energy which proceeds from its radiant form is thought of, rather than the form itself. This energy is of electric nature and from its fusion with the magnetic energy of the Sun it is expanded into a great spheric globe which surrounds and interpenetrates the denser sphere called *Earth*. It gives the power of creation to the forces developing throughout the Sun system. It has been likened to a great womb; hence it is called the *female* or *mother* principle of the universe. In the process of creation the seven life Forces lay quiescent in the matrix of the great Mother Venus, until in the fullness of their maturity they emerged to begin a new cycle of growth. So you see that the realm of Venus is much more than a star, as you have conceived it, an unrelated lantern hanging in the ether, perhaps. The spark you see and call a *planet* is the point of contact between the positive energy of the Sun and the negative energy Venus. But for Venus, the female or Soul principle, whose symbol is the element Water, which has been called the *subconscious realm of life*, the little ones who dwell in the realm of Earth could never create a poem, a song, or a child.

I, Sano Tarot, who govern the Venus sphere
of life, say this, which is truth.

Singers of harmony songs find the road to peace. The road to peace is found by those who know their own singing mates and sing the songs which vibrate through the universe and find their sister songs on the heights of spiritual expansion. The Seers on the heights of spiritual expansion issue the order that the singers of songs of Tarot use the ancient Egyptian method of concentration to find their places in the universe that harmony may settle like a dove upon them.

The ancient Egyptian method of concentration places the mind on the navel, this being the eye of the solar plexus which is the center of life in the physical body. This center places the right Forces on the right planes to develop the spiritual side of themselves. On the physical side, the solar plexus gives the body the inspiration to live.

The navel center may be likened to the Sun, whose everlasting fire stirs the dormant Forces in the realm of Earth. The fire of the navel center mates the physical Forces of the solar plexus, and from this polarity expansion proceeds.[3]

This Egyptian method of concentration is the best method known to hold stillness in the physical body that the life Forces may expand and contact the spiritual Forces which make music of harmony in the disciple's life. The solar plexus sings to the physical and issues the order of balancing the physical and the spiritual Forces. Sing to the solar plexus, and you will see and hear things hidden from men on the physical side of life. The things of the spirit sing the song of eternal life.

The peace which passes understanding comes when songs are sung through the finding of the center of life in the body. This center is found through the balancing of the navel plexus on the spiritual side with the solar plexus on the physical side. Issue the

---

[3] The navel center may be likened to the positive or male principle and the solar plexus to the negative or female principle. The negative Forces expand only through impregnation by the positive Forces. It will require both courage and strength of character to make wise use of the new influx of life which will result from the conscious awakening of the creative Forces dormant in man. I speak only to the strong.

Sano Tarot.

command of the gods that the disciple on the road to peace use concentration as directed. Breathe deeply and center the attention on the navel and request the spirit of Love to show you the way to find the realm to which you belong that you may sing its song and overcome the tone of discord which resounds in your own song. The overcoming of the tone of discord in the lives of the people brings about the songs of harmony in the universe. The discord comes from trying to sing in realms other than your own. *Find your own octave and sound your note on its vibration.*

I, Sano Tarot, have spoken.

Hear me, Sano Tarot:

Harps of golden tones make music and sing songs of inspiration to the Seers who sing their songs on their own vibrating note. Right royally do they reverberate on the spiritual heights of their vibration. Heights undreamed of by those who dwell on the physical planes of expression are reached on the spiritual planes above them when songs are sung on the note vibrating to the notes of their singing mates. Songs on the spiritual side of life singing to their mates on the physical side bring tones of wondrous beauty.

Hear me, Sano Tarot:

In the days of singing mates in the realm of Venus, only the right Forces sang together. The right songs sung by the right singing mates made the universe ring with harmony.

Hear me, Sano Tarot:

The cause of the separation of the Forces was the Free Will given to them by the King, who desired their further development in their own realms. Such was their joy over the gift of the King that they vied with each other as to who should inspire the most songs from the Forces about them. Songs became discordant, and the King drove them from his sphere of harmony. The Forces, mad with freedom, sang of other spheres; so the King sang to their dismissal, and they hurled themselves out of the kingdom of Love, and the force of their fall formed the planet Earth, the planet singing to discord.

I, Sano Tarot, have spoken.

Singers on the Earth planet have always sung songs of inharmony. But singers on the Earth planet may inspire harmony if they sing only on their own planes of expression in their own realms of being. Sing the song of Tarot and enter the royal road to peace!

Hear me, Sano Tarot:
Gano Tarot sings the song of Universal Love and the brotherhood of man. Then let all the people who sing the Gano Tarot song sing only of Universal Love, and no other song shall they sing.

Rano Tarot sings the song of Faith in the universe. Then let all the people who sing the Rano Tarot song sing of Faith in the universe, and no other song shall they sing.

I, Sano Tarot, sing of Inspiration. Then let all the people who sing the Sano Tarot song sing of Inspiration, and no other song shall they sing.

Tano Tarot sings the song of Material Wealth. Then let all the people who sing the Tano Tarot song sing of Material Wealth, and no other song shall they sing.

Fano Tarot sings of Heart. Then let all the people who sing the Fano Tarot song sing of Heart, and no other song shall they sing.

Pano Taro sings of Spiritual Mind. Then let all the people who sing the Pano Tarot song sing only of Spiritual Mind, and no other song shall they sing.

Ono Tarot sings the song of Hope. Then let all the people who sing the Ono Tarot song sing of Hope, and no other song shall they sing.

Sing the song of Tarot and enter the royal road to peace.

I, Sano Tarot, have spoken.

The songs of Tarot are the vibrations of balanced Forces. The singers are those who vibrate in their own realms of being and who issue the order of the spiritual Forces to sing with the physical

Forces on their own planes of development. Songs sung by the right singers on their own planes of development mate the songs of the universe in harmony.

Hope is the song of all realms. The song of Hope heals the sick and lifts the downcast. Hope is the healing force of the planet Earth. It sings of everlasting life. It fills the singers of songs of discord with the feeling of better things to come. Right royally, it saves them from despair. The song of Hope rises high above the songs of singers of death, and right royally has it saved the race from destruction. Singing to itself, it sings the sexless song of the universe. The sexless songs sing only to themselves.

I, Sano Tarot, have spoken.

The song of the sexes is the song of Love. The song of Love is the song of harmony, and harmony is found only when the singers are on their own plane of development in their own realms of being. Sing the songs of harmony and enter the royal road to peace.

I, Sano Tarot, have spoken.

Hear me, Sano Tarot:

Sing to the right mates on their own planes if you would find peace. Only those on the same plane of development in their own realm of being should inspire each other. Singers on other planes than their own sing to destruction and death. Singers of songs of destruction and death are the souls of those who sing on other planes than their own. The songs of singers on their own planes of development in their own realms of being are the songs of the harmony and beauty of the spheres. Then, and only then, do the angels cry aloud their hymns of praise to the great Gano Tarot, who seals their union with his approval.

I, Sano Tarot, have spoken.

The overcoming of the flesh is the highest test of the disciple on the road to peace. Riches of the Earth and of the spirit are for those who sing the songs of harmony. Utter destruction is for those who sing the songs of inharmony. The songs of harmony ring high in the heavens. The songs of inharmony toll the bell of sorrow on the Earth planet. Sing with the singers of harmony and tread the royal road to peace.

Hear me, Sano Tarot:

Sing the song of spiritual union, and the great Gano Tarot will hear your prayer. But the cry of singers far apart, he cannot hear. The singers themselves place songs of sadness in the hearts of each other, and their songs cannot rise above the tones of sorrow. Hence they do not reach the high place of the great Gano Tarot, where only harmony reigns.

I, Sano Tarot, have spoken.

Hear me, Sano Tarot:

I say that singers of sorrow on the Earth planet sing on the wrong planes of expression in the wrong realms of being. They should concentrate and hear the song of their own plane of development in their own realms. Then they should time their songs to the vibrations of their planes, and lo, harmony will sing its song of joy and take away the sting of singing to the wrong mate. Let all who sing songs of sorrow insist that their singing mates be found that life may yield its sweetest songs on the planet Earth. Right royally, the songs of the right singing mates may be heard through the practice of balanced concentration as taught by Tarot.[4]

---

[4] Give close ear to me that I may make clear to you the principle of balanced concentration. It is the part of wisdom to give thought to a new problem which presents itself to you. Know you this: the seven life Forces center in the solar plexus and lie dormant there until they are awakened by the positive force which dwells in the navel center. Man is a replica of the universe, and the navel plexus is the Sun. It may be of assistance to illustrate the solar plexus as the base or foundation of a house. Now the house is steady or not according to the balance of its foundation stones. This center of Forces is the cornerstone of the temple not made with hands, which is your body. This cornerstone must express life, for what does it profit a man if his foundation be dead and crumbling? Life more abundant is the reward of him who knows the

Hear me, Sano Tarot:

 I say that the singing mates may be found through balanced concentration. Riches of the Earth and of the Spirit are bound together in the song of Tarot. The song of Tarot is the song of peace. The song of peace is the singing on your own plane of development in your own realm of being. Sing the song of Tarot and find the royal road to peace.

Hear Sano Tarot, who has spoken.

Hope is a sexless Force and belongs to all planes alike. It is the seed or leaven of the universe from which life springs. The Force of Hope lights the dark places of Earth and sings to the saving of the people. The song of Hope inspires the hearts of the people to sing of new life on the planet Earth. Hope sings the joy of healing.

---

law of balance and uses it. I say to you that the Forces dormant in the solar plexus become active only through impregnation by the positive force which centers in the navel. Therefore you see that concentration on the navel quickens the action of the seven primal Forces vibrating there, and according to his use of his awakened Forces does man lift himself toward the fulfillment of his destiny. The simple knowledge that you have found the center of life in your body should give you sufficient illumination for practice. Bring your consciousness to your navel as the center of balance in your body. This is all you need to do. Straining to visualize the point is of no value, for it is thus that the mind confuses intuition. The intellect plays no part in the recognition of the life center in the navel. Bear in mind that you are dealing with vital Forces which express themselves as principles and not as physical forms. The mind forms pictures out of its own stuff, which oft-times are totally untrue. It is the deep knowledge that the Forces which build your whole expression of life center here that will awaken these Forces to their full expression. Let the Spirit within you glow with consciousness that you have found the cornerstone of your life's expression, and proceed to live from this center, rather than from your mental realm which you must know is the servant of the Spirit which dwells in the Sun center of your body. Speak the word of willing service, then move forward as your intuition directs, for it is through intuition that the Spirit will guide you. Concentrating on the navel center polarizes the positive and negative Forces in your body, thus making a channel of balanced Forces through which intuition sings with clear vision.

It sings the song of sorrow's overcoming. It binds the wounds of singers to pain and heals their scars. Sing the song of Tarot and find the road to peace.

Hear Sano Tarot, who has spoken!

Join the right singers on the right planes, and Hope will nest on their songs, and they will soar to the sphere of harmony. Sing the song of Tarot and enter the realm of Hope! Together the songs of the right mates will inspire the song of Hope. The song of Hope will lift the songs of the people of Earth, and they will reach the harmony sphere of the Great Gano Tarot.

Sano Tarot has spoken.

Together singers of songs on their own planes of development in their own realms of being sing of Seers' Inspiration. The Inspiration of the Seers means the clear vision of those who have earned seership by the overcoming of the flesh in their own realms of being. The Seers are a privileged people, for they have served the race on their own planes of development. The Seers inspire the race to higher calling. They toll the bell of sadness when songs are sung by the wrong mates on the wrong planes of expression. The Seers sing only to their own mates and inspire them to reach the heights of spiritual expansion. Sing songs of inspiration to the Seers on the heights of spiritual expansion.

Hear Sano Tarot, who has spoken!

Songs of Seers' inspiration form the choir invisible of Gano's Tarot's realm of Universal Love. Here the songs ring out in beauty, issued by the Great Gano Tarot himself. Heard on the Earth planet, they bring the peace which passes understanding to those who have ears to hear. Sing the song of Seers' inspiration and hear the song of peace.

I, Sano Tarot, have spoken.

The inspiration of the Seers is the overcoming of the flesh on their own planes and the song of victory. Inspiration of the Seers on their own plane means the victory over some sin of the flesh. This places the disciple on his own plane of vibration in the position he has earned in this and past lives.

Hear Sano Tarot, who has spoken!

The Seers are the people who have overcome the flesh on their own planes and have not tried to do the work which other planes inspire. The Seers inspire their own planes of expression and no other.

Hear me, Sano Tarot:

Inspiration of the Seers means the singing to the expression of your own Tarot, or place in which you stand in your soul's development. Sing to your own place, and you will sing to harmony. The songs of souls on their own planes of development resound to beauty and sweetness.

Souls singing on their own planes give ear to their own vibrations. Their own vibrations are their mates. Songs sung by singers on their own planes vibrate themselves to higher planes. Sing your own song and feel its joy.

I, Sano Tarot, have spoken.

The songs of Gano Tarot are the songs of Universal Love. The songs of the Universal Love of Gano Tarot are the songs which tune their notes to the Universal Love songs of Earth.

The songs of Rano Tarot are the songs which sing of Faith.

The songs which vibrate to Sano Tarot are the songs of Inspiration.

The songs which are heard in the realm of Tano Tarot have their mates in the realm of Material Wealth.

The vibration of Fano Tarot resounds to the love of service — the righting of the wrongs of the people.

The singers of Pano Tarot find their response in the realm of Mind.

The rhythm of the Ono Tarot realm issues the order of Hope.

The plane on which the disciple stands is determined by the song he sings on his plane of expression. When he sings the song of other planes than his own, he retrogrades on the road to peace, and nothing can save him until he finds his own plane and sings thereon. The disciple expressing on other planes than his own should use balanced concentration, requesting the great Gano Tarot to show him his own plane that he may tune his song to its vibration. The disciple creates his own plane by the deeds he has done and the thoughts he has allowed to enter his consciousness.

Hear me, Sano Tarot:

The deeds of the body and the mind give tone to the song the disciple sings and place him on the plane he deserves. His place on the royal road to peace is determined by concentration. Concentration sings to the spiritual realm and, through the balanced channel of intuition, shows him the plane he has earned. Concentration sings the song of knowledge.

Hear me, Sano Tarot:

The neophyte is one whose vibrations are not of such height that he can respond to vibration of rare swift nature. The song of the neophyte is the song of material will. Then let all neophytes sing of material will, thus working on their own planes which will lift them into Tarot or the higher law. To enter Tarot means to have found the royal road to peace. This road is situated in the royal temple grounds. The temple vibrates to the Gano Tarot realm, which is the realm of Universal Love. The Dove of Peace sings to the temple and vies with Gano Tarot to sing with the people of Earth.

I, Sano Tarot, have spoken.

The songs of the Gano Tarot realm are the songs of Love. They sing to the peace of the people of Earth. Gano Tarot issues the order that his people sing only to him, and right royally, he promises them peace. He bids them use concentration that they may hear his songs of peace and sing them in the realm of Earth.

Songs of Rano Tarot are the songs of the Faith principle in the universe. Rano Tarot issues the order that his people sing only to him.

Sano Tarot sings the songs of Inspiration. He hears only the song of his people in the realm of Earth.

Tano Tarot sings the song of Material Wealth and hears no song but his own.

Fano Tarot sings to the Heart Force and listens only when his own songs vibrate to him.

Pano Tarot sings to the Force of Mind and issues the order that no song shall reach him save his own.

Ono Tarot sings of Hope, the one and all. His music makes the leaven in which the seed of life expands. All the Forces respond to its song.

The disciple must find the One whose song he sings and issue the order to himself that he will sing no other. The singers of songs other than their own sing to discord and death.

I, Sano Tarot, have spoken.

Hear me, Sano Tarot:

Songs of singers in the realm of Earth must resound their tones in their own realms of expression in their own realms of being.

Through concentration as directed, the physical and the spiritual sides of life issue the order of balance and sing together.

Issue the order to yourselves, children of Earth, that you sing the song of balanced Forces. The song of balance is the song of vision, and you will see and know the right song to sing to bring harmony into your music.

The songs of Tarot are the songs of balance and peace. Concentrate and find your position in the universe. Sing on the right plane, and you will find peace.

I, Sano Tarot, have spoken.

2. THE SEXES ON THE ROYAL ROAD TO PEACE

The sex principle is the only principle which governs the spiritual growth of the people on the planes of their development. Right royally, the sex force contributes to the joining of the spiritual and physical Forces. Polarized Forces sing the song of peace. The singers toll the bell of death on their own planes when the sexes unite on other planes than their own. Songs sung on the wrong planes of expression by the wrong mates kill the spiritual vibrations.

Order in the realm of sex issues the right royal songs of harmony on Earth. Riches of the spiritual and the physical are for those who sing on the right sex planes. The sex principle is the song of life. The sexes are but halves of themselves. The sex force is divided into songs of male and female. Together they form the whole song singing to peace and do vie with life to sing with them.

Hear me, Sano Tarot:
The sex force sings of life. Together the sexes sing of service to mankind. Service is the highest privilege of the sexes. Sing to the right mating of the sexes, and you have sung to the service of mankind.

I, Sano Tarot, have spoken.

Join the right sex Forces and the planet Earth reaps a rich reward. Join the wrong sex Forces, and the planet reaps destruction and death. Together the right sex Forces sing of growth. Together the wrong sex Forces sing to killing the spirit within the singers. The killing of the spirit means the killing of life on Earth. Vie with the sexes to sing on their own planes is the message of Tarot.

I, Sano Tarot, have spoken.

Hear me, Sano Tarot:
I say that error on the sex planes issues the order of misery in the hearts of the people. The only hope of singers on the Earth planet is in the right mating of the right Forces. The singers of

harmony find their mates in the singers of their own songs. Join the mates on the right planes, and life will sing with the harmony of the spheres. Vie with overcoming the wrong Forces, and Gano Tarot will hear your prayer and overcome the discord in your own song. Join the right Forces, and you will have taken the sorrow from the song of Earth. Singers of sorrow, join the right Forces and sing the song of joy. Welcome the song, singers of sorrow, and receive the peace which passes understanding.

I, Sano Tarot, have spoken.

The seven realms of being have seven lesser realms. Each realm issues the order of sex. In the realm of spirit, the sexes know their sister Forces, and the sister Forces know their mates. The spiritual force of the Sun mates the physical force of the soil, and lo, the law of growth is expressed. So the spiritual mates the physical, and harmony prevails.

The law of harmony sings of Forces uniting on the right planes of expression in their right realms of being. Then, and only then, can harmony sing. The whole universe is based on sex force.

Hear me, Sano Tarot:

In the realm of spirit, the sexes light the dark places of Earth. Their united Forces join the physical with the spiritual.

I, Sano Tarot, have spoken.

The sex Forces in the seven realms of being sing their own songs on their own planes of expression. Together, they sing of life. Separated, they sing of death. The sex question is the most vital one before the race today. Great souls are being hurled to destruction by Forces not in harmony with themselves.

Hear me, Sano Tarot:

The sex Force of the planet Earth hears the call of Gano Tarot in that it serves the race with new life. It sends the order of creation to the mates who are singing their own songs on their own planes. Only the singers of their own songs feel new life in their singing.

Sing to the new life of the planet Earth, and you will sing to Gano Tarot. Vie with the Forces of sex to overcome death and create new life. Issue the order that the songs of the planet resound the notes of new life, and the echo of their music will reach the great Gano Tarot, and he will bring order in the lives of the singers. He will join the physical and the spiritual Forces in their own realms of being and make music of harmony sublime.

Join the right sex Forces in the right realms of being and sing the song of balance and beauty.

I, Sano Tarot, have spoken.

Tie the Forces of the singers in the right realms of being and hear the voice of Gano Tarot. The singers of harmony are singers of sweetest tones, like the issuing of the music of the spheres.

I, Sano Tarot, have spoken.

The Seers on the heights of spiritual expansion sing songs of joy. Their songs of joy send their tones through the universe, straight into the hearts of singers of harmony in the realm of Earth. Forces of sex harmony join the songs of the Seers on the heights to the songs of singers of harmony, and lo, the planet Earth trembles with the ecstasy of Gano Tarot's realm of Love.

In the realm of Gano Tarot, the sex Forces issue the order of service to the race. Service to the race can be given only in harmony. In harmony, the realm of Universal Love sings to the planet Earth. It sings the song of peace and issues the order of the overcoming of sorrow. Vie with the right sex Forces to sing on their own planes. Tie the right sex Forces to the harmony realm and Gano Tarot will hear your prayer for harmony in your own song and serve the race by the ordering of new life in its song.

I, Sano Tarot, have spoken.

3. THE ROYAL ROAD TO PEACE THROUGH SERVICE OF THE RACE

The song of service issues the highest note in the music of the spheres. It is heard resounding through all planes of expression in all realms of being. Singers of service mate the notes of the universe and sing the harmony song through the joining of the right Forces in the right realms of being.

I, Sano Tarot, have spoken.

Issue the order of service to the race by joining the right Forces together. The songs of balanced Forces issue the order of Universal Love. With each song sung by the right Forces, the sorrow of Earth is lessened. Together the songs of the spiritual and physical Forces tell the story of Gano Tarot's realm on the planet Earth. The song of Gano Tarot is the song of brotherhood through the song of Universal Love.

I, Sano Tarot, have spoken.

Hear me, Sano Tarot:
I say that the song of Gano Tarot is the song of brotherhood through Universal Love, and through Universal Love will the song of brotherhood he heard on the planet Earth.

Hear me, Sano Tarot:
Love is the only song of Gano Tarot's realm. Vie with Gano Tarot to sing his song of Love on the planet Earth, that the song of brotherhood may tune its notes with the Gano Tarot song.

Hear me, Sano Tarot:
Faith is the song of the Rano Tarot realm. Vie with Rano Tarot that his song of Faith may tune its note to the song of service on the Earth planet. Together the song of Faith and the song of Love will sing the song of brotherhood.

Hear me, Sano Tarot:
  I say that the song of Love and the song of Faith together will sing the song of brotherhood.
  I, Sano Tarot, have spoken.

Hear me, Sano Tarot:
  Hope is the healing Force of the planet Earth, and Hope, together with Love and Faith, sings of service to the race. Tones of wondrous sweetness rise to Gano Tarot's realm when Love, Faith, and Hope sing together.
  I, Sano Tarot, have spoken.

Hear me, Sano Tarot:
  The right royal tone of Sano Tarot issues the note of Inspiration to the race. The tone of Inspiration sung through the songs of Love, Faith, and Hope makes music of harmony. Singers of harmony songs serve the race on the planet Earth.
  I, Sano Tarot, have spoken.

Hear me, Sano Tarot:
  The song of Tano Tarot sings of Material Wealth. The song of Material Wealth stirs the people to use their power and sing to the service of the race. The tone of Material Wealth ringing through the songs of Love, Faith, Hope, and Inspiration issues a song of sweetest music through the spheres of singers on the planet Earth.
  I, Sano Tarot, have spoken.

Hear me, Sano Tarot:
  Singers of songs of Fano Tarot sing of Heart, issuing the order of righting the wrongs of the people of Earth. The singers of Fano Tarot songs will hear the music issuing from the realms of Love, Faith, Hope, Inspiration, and Material Wealth. The singers will sing with new tones of sweetness and strength, and right royally will the race be served.
  I, Sano Tarot, have spoken.

Hear me, Sano Tarot:

Pano Tarot sings of Spiritual Mind. His songs will be heard through the sweetness of the service songs issued by the seven realms of being on the planet Earth.

I, Sano Tarot, have spoken.

Hear me, Sano Tarot:

The service song can be sung only when the singers vibrate on their own planes of expression in their own realms of being. The singers of songs of service sing only their own songs. Only their own songs can be heard in the service song of the universe. Vie with your own plane of expression in your own realm of being if you would sing in the harmony song, which rises to the realm of Universal Love. The song of harmony makes music issue from all planes of expression. Harmony issuing from all planes of expression will make the planet Earth utter the sweetest songs of life and love. Sing to Gano Tarot and listen to the music you have made. Join the songs of Love to the songs issuing the same tones on the same plane of vibration in the same Tarot of their development. Join their wings, and they will fly together in the sunlight. Join the tones of their songs, and they will resound the music of Universal Love.

I, Sano Tarot, have spoken.

Hear me, Sano Tarot:

Issuing the music of the Gano Tarot realm rings the bell of peace on Earth. Peace on Earth comes only to those ringing the bell in Gano Tarot's realm. No song sung out of the Gano Tarot realm will resound the peace which passes understanding. The music of Gano Tarot can vibrate only through perfect mates. Overcome the flesh and hear the perfect mating song of Gano Tarot. The perfect mates are the perfect Forces joined together on their own planes of expression in their own realms. Sing the song of perfect mates and hear the music of their song.

Issue the order to the people to insist that their mates be found. Then join their physical and spiritual Forces and ring the bell of service to the race.

I, Sano Tarot, have spoken.

Light sings the masculine song, and Dark makes feminine music. Join the male Light to the female Dark, and lo, there sings the song of growth. Either force alone would sing to destruction and death. Rich music of mellow tones sounds in the Earth's seasons. Their sex force sings to planting and harvesting. Issue the order that the seasons sing their song of sex that the race may be served through the increase. The seasons sing the song of growth, and all the race is served.

Hear me, Sano Tarot:

I say that the seasons sing the song of growth, and all the race is served. The music of the seasons tells the story of mates singing together in harmony. Sing songs of harmony and make the music of the spheres.

I, Sano Tarot, have spoken.

Hear me, Sano Tarot:

Knowledge issues music of harmony. Songs sung in harmony overcome the discord on the planet Earth. Songs of knowledge make music of harmony. Sing the song of service through the knowledge of spiritual law. Issue the order that knowledge vie with the overcoming of songs sung through the misunderstanding of Tarot. The tones of knowledge sound in the realm of service. Make music of knowledge and serve the race!

I, Sano Tarot, have spoken.

Join the songs of service with the songs of sex and issue the order of knowledge. Through knowledge, songs of richness will be heard. Mate the songs of service, sex, and knowledge on the planet Earth and Gano Tarot's realm will be realized. The realization of Gano Tarot's realm means the reign of balanced Forces.

Love is the highest earthly song. The tones of Love issue the song of life on all planes of expression. The song of Love joins the songs of service, sex, and knowledge in the great choir invisible. Join the songs of service, sex, and knowledge together, and the race will be saved from destruction.

I, Sano Tarot, have spoken.

Light is the sexual mate of Dark. Together they sing of days and nights. Their song sings of Gano Tarot's realm of Love in that he hears their prayer and joins their forces, which brings forth another day.

Dry is the mate of Wet. Their song sings to Gano Tarot in that he hears their cry and joins their forces, and they bring forth moisture.

Hear me, Sano Tarot:
I say that Gano Tarot hears the cry of the Forces and answers their prayer.

I, Sano Tarot, have spoken.

Sex force issues the order of growth. Growth sings of sex harmony on Earth. The overcoming of sex inharmony means the mating of the Forces on their own planes of expression in their own realms of being, thus joining the physical and the spiritual Forces. Through the polarization of the spiritual and physical Forces, the heart of Love beats through the heart of Hope.

Hear Sano Tarot, who has spoken.

Tears of sorrow are shed over the singers on the wrong sex planes. They hear only the wail of desire unsatisfied. The wail of desire unsatisfied means the sex force gone awry without the seal of Gano Tarot's approval. Only the songs sung by the singers on their own plane of vibration bear the seal of Gano Tarot's approval and issue the peace which passes understanding.

Hear me, Sano Tarot:

The songs which bear the seal of Gano Tarot's approval send their tones through the universe as light sends its rays. The rays light the dark places and reach the uttermost ends of Earth. So the songs fill the air with the music of the spheres, and Gano Tarot joins the physical Forces with the spiritual Forces and seals their union with his approval. The rays of light which penetrate the ether hear the voice of sex on their own planes. The force of sex is the force of new life. It sings in the plants; it mates the sunlight with the dark Earth, and lo, songs of new growth are heard through the universe. Give ear to the voice of the plane on which you sing and its sister voices, and you will sing to harmony in your new growth. Overcome the singing of Light and Dark together, and you have sung to destruction and death. Only the right Forces singing together can sing songs of new growth. Overcome Dark and issue the order that Light sing alone, and the song of Light will die. The songs of the universe must mate their complementary songs or toll the bell on their lives. Issue the order that no song shall sing alone.

Sing the song of perfect mates and hear the music of the spheres. The song of Tarot sings to perfect mates on the planet Earth. The song of perfect mates vibrates to the harmony of the spheres, and the song of the harmony of the spheres makes music of the peace which passes understanding.

I, Sano Tarot, have spoken.

4. THE TIMEKEEPER ON THE ROYAL ROAD TO PEACE

Horns of plenty fill the songs of singers in the right realms of being. The horn of plenty is the reward of singers who sing only their own songs.

Hear me, Sano Tarot:
   I say that the horn of plenty is the reward of singers who sing in their own realms of being. Together the singers overcome the songs not their own and join their Forces in the realm of Earth. They take time by the forelock and insist that they find their complements on all planes of expression and so avoid the bitter result of singing songs not their own. Mate the right Forces on the right planes and receive the outpouring of the horn of plenty. The overcoming of poverty is the song of the horn of plenty. Together the right Forces sing to the horn of plenty.

I, Sano Tarot, have spoken.

Hear me, Sano Tarot:
   In the spiritual realm, there is plenty for all. Vie with the Timekeeper to toll the bell on singing to poverty and hear the note of the horn of plenty. In the spiritual realm, the horn of plenty blows tones of glorious music.

Hear me, Sano Tarot:
   I say that in the spiritual realm, the horn of plenty blows tones of glorious music! Out of the mouth of the horn of plenty, there sounds a royal blast. Only those whose notes are tuned to its harmony can hear its wondrous beauty.

I, Sano Tarot, have spoken.

Time was with space when the Forces of the universe made music with their own instruments and sang the harmony song in their own homes. Time was not with them, nor was space. Only the present was their guide. Then the King gave his Forces the gift of Free Will whereby they might expand in their own realms in the scheme of making a world of peace and plenty.

I, Sano Tarot, have spoken.

Hear the Timekeeper!

I, the Timekeeper, saw from afar the result of the gift of Free Will to the Forces, in that they would misuse the freedom given to them and lose control of the spiritual will already theirs. I saw that they would lust after the power of other Forces in other realms. Free Will vied with the King as to who should rule, and the Forces vied with him to overcome the King. The King heard their cry against him and ordered that they hear only his voice or depart from his realm of harmony. Utter consternation reigned, and Free Will bade the Forces to do as they would with each other, and they, being mad with freedom, reached out and overcame other realms than their own. Again the King ordered that they leave the overcoming of other realms to him, but the mad Forces heeded him not, for they had been told by Free Will that the mating of all the Forces was their right. They joined their Forces with the Forces of other realms, and the King dismissed them from his kingdom. They fell from their high estate, and the force of their fall formed a new realm in the universe — a realm composed of discordant Forces.

The force of the Moon, which had never vied with disobedience, heard the cry of the hurling Forces and reached out and joined them, thus breaking the law of balance in her own realm of being. Her spirit fled, and she was left with only her physical force. Her spirit vied with the Sun to save her from destruction. The Sun drew close, and the Moon told her story to him. Free Will commanded that they join their forces, and on the day of their union, light dawned in the chaotic realm of Earth. The Moon gave the Sun her dead body, and the Sun revived it with his spiritual Fire, and she became the medium through which the spirit of the King entered the chaotic realm of Earth. But for the union of the spiritual and physical forces of the Sun and the Moon, the planet Earth must have died.

The Timekeeper has spoken.

Hear me, Sano Tarot:

I say that the Timekeeper speaks truth. By my order, he will tell the story of mates in the kingdom of harmony.

In the kingdom of harmony, the Forces were in the right condition to join themselves together and form the perfect sphere of balanced Forces, which was the King's plan of creation. Harmony was its keynote, and their years were the present, for there was no past and no future. Service was their watchword and love was their reason for being.

The Timekeeper has spoken.

Moreover, the Timekeeper speaks truth when he says that love was their reason for being. O my people, join with the Timekeeper and tell the story of service and love! Service is the Law of Love. The Timekeeper will resume the story.

Sano Tarot has spoken.

Hear me, the Timekeeper:

When the King saw that his Forces were growing too self-satisfied, he knew that they were ripe for further expansion, so he told them that he would make them a gift, and with it, they might grow into gods themselves. Joining the spiritual Forces with the physical Forces was the gift he planned for them. It would give them the power of reproduction and make them gods indeed.

Hear me, Sano Tarot:

I say that the power of reproduction makes gods of men only when the spiritual and physical Forces join through the medium of perfect balance. The medium of perfect balance is found only when the Forces issue the call of separation to their mates, and their mates hear the call and respond. The King signs his approval only upon such unions and gives the joining Forces the power to create beings in their own image and in the image of the King.

Forces in the sphere of harmony, not having joined their spiritual and physical sides, had not the power to reproduce themselves. Such was their content that they refused to advance in spiritual or physical expansion. When the King told them of the gift he was giving them, they went wild with joy and soon began to use their power to bring into existence beings on other planes than their own, and the expansion of their own Forces ceased to express harmony and growth. The King remonstrated with them, but they listened not. He ordered them to expand their Forces only in their own realms of being, but they heeded him not until they heard his voice saying: "Depart, all ye who refuse to do my bidding!"

Some heard and returned to their Father's realm, others refused to obey, and the King drove them from his kingdom of harmony and forbade their return until they were willing to reproduce themselves only in their own realms of being. So, until this day, the rebellious children of the King have wandered over the face of the Earth without the seal of the King's approval on the union of their Forces. Only when they heed his voice and obey his command can they return to his kingdom of love and harmony.

I, Sano Tarot, have spoken.

By my order, the Timekeeper will now tell the story of the overcoming.

Sano Tarot.

The Forces in the kingdom of harmony overcame the Forces in other realms than their own, which caused their separation and discord. The Force of Mind overcame the Force of Heart, and from the union of their Forces came a child of inharmony.

The Force of Inspiration heard the call of Faith with no regard for the law of balance, and they created a being without Heart or Mind.

The Force of Universal Love heard the call of Heart, and they joined the right planes of their expression, and Harmony is their child.

The Force of Material Wealth heard no call but its own, but all the Forces hear its call and reach for its barren self.

Such confusion of the Forces caused their downfall. Harmony comes only when the King seals the union of mates with his approval, and this approval is given only when the Forces of the spiritual and the physical are joined on their own planes of development in their own realm of being.

The Timekeeper has spoken.

Hear me, Sano Tarot:

The Timekeeper has spoken truth. Vie with him to tell the story of the King's plan, which was overthrown by the disobedient Forces.

Sano Tarot.

I, the Timekeeper, say that the King's plan was the perfect one of allowing each Force to work out its own expansion in its own realm with the Forces which harmonized with it. This was the King's hope. His plan would have answered all the desires of the Forces of his kingdom, and he was hurt beyond belief when his hitherto obedient children turned from his love and rebelled against his rule. His plan would have joined the right spiritual Forces with the right physical Forces, and gods they would have been — gods of creation on their own planes and gods of their own realms of harmony. Vie with Sano Tarot to tell you of the kingdom as the King would have had it.

The Timekeeper has spoken.

Imagine a song of perfect harmony floating upward and answering itself through the air, the sea, and the Earth, which resound its beauty and return it in perfect accord. Join the right Forces in the right realms of being, and this song may still be heard on the planet Earth. Joining the right Forces is the King's way of singing songs of harmony, which blend their notes and make the music of peace send its tone through the universe.

The King's realm was such as this. He sang the song of love and listened to the return of its vibration. He issued the order that his song should answer itself and then make more music of its kind. Sweet accord sounded through his realm like music from harps of gold. Songs of rich and royal tones floated out from his kingdom, sounding the note of his vibration which gave them the color of rarest tints. Their hues vied with one another as to which should show the greatest beauty in the kingdom. The same wealth which gave them color gave harmony to their songs. Free Will was not among them. The will of the King was their law, and he ruled them with loving-kindness.

The Timekeeper will finish the story of the Forces. He remembers well the sad fate of the kingdom of harmony.

Right royal Sano Tarot, correct notes have been my guide in speaking. Utter desolation overcame the kingdom of harmony when the Forces rebelled and elected to live under the ride of Free Will. I say that utter desolation overcame the kingdom of harmony, and only the Forces which remained true to their own realms remained with the King after he drove his disobedient children out of his kingdom.

Hear me, Sano Tarot:
That which the Timekeeper speaks is truth.

Without the right Forces to serve him, the King became sad, and only when he vied with Ono Tarot to save them did his hope revive. His sorrow was lessened by Hope, and he made an agreement with his Forces which had not failed him, that at given periods of time, as time is counted by the Earth people, he would again give them the opportunity of re-entering the kingdom of harmony without which they would disintegrate. Many periods of like measure have passed, and the King has never failed to send new light to his mistaken children when the period has finished its cycle of expression, and many children have seen the light and returned to their Father's house.

Such a period of time is now drawing to a close. A new cycle of time is in its inception, bringing light and understanding of spiritual law. Be among those who sense the light. Issue the command that now the people join their Forces on the right planes of expression in their own realms of being, and new life will be given to the children of the King, wandering in the darkness which ignorance makes its own.

Vie with the children of the King to obey the command of the King and return to their joyous inheritance.

I, Sano Tarot, have spoken.

5. THE FORCES ON THE ROAD TO PEACE

Hear me, Sano Tarot:

I speak in the name of the Forces which are expanding in the realm of Earth, where sex issues the order of the growth and polarization of themselves, in the making of a perfect sphere of balanced Forces. The gods take great care that only the right Forces join their spiritual and physical Sides in the great scheme of harmonious expansion.

In the spiritual realm, the Force of Universal Love is masculine and balances itself only with the feminine Forces of the universe.

The Force of Faith is masculine and calls the feminine Forces of the universe.

The Force of Inspiration is feminine and answers the call of the masculine Forces in the universe.

The Force of Material Wealth is balanced and gives itself freely by expansion.

The Force of Heart in the realm of service is feminine and mates only the masculine Forces in the universe.

The Force of Spiritual Mind is masculine and seeks only the feminine Forces in the universe.

The Force of Hope is balanced and gives itself as the seed whereby all realms of being expand.

Join the right Forces on the right planes of expression, and the King will hear your prayer for harmony, and right royally will he answer it. Vie with the Timekeeper to tell the story of the milestones or lesser vibratory laws through which the gods lead the seekers after truth.

I, Sano Tarot, have spoken.

I, the Timekeeper, say that each of the seven great primal Forces is divided into seven degrees of itself through which the disciple expands and balances his expression of life. As his consciousness expands, the first change in his vibratory movement is called:

The Rope Walker's degree, which means the balancing of thought force in a new vibration.

The Reader's degree, which means that the disciple has assimilated the new state of consciousness given by the Rope Walker's vibration.

The Saint's degree, which means that the disciple has now raised his vibration so that he can sense the spiritual side of the degree he is expressing.

The Seer's Insignia degree, which means that the disciple has so balanced and expanded his Forces that he can overlook the future of his own expanding Forces.

The Purple Order degree, which means mastery of the disciple's own plane of expression. Here he can consciously use his Forces for his own benefit.

The degree of Seers in Higher Vibration, which means that the disciple has now earned the privilege of seeing the royal road which he has trod and the spiritual height which is his goal.

The degree of High Priest, which means that the disciple has balanced his life Forces in the Tarot he is expressing and is ready for development in a higher realm.

These vibrations are the seven gates which open the way to the garden of roses in the temple grounds.

I, the Timekeeper, have spoken.

I, Sano Tarot, say that the chemistry of life is indeed profound.

Light is the mate of Dark, and the King will give Light his wish to save the realm of Earth from disintegration when he joins his force to hers in full completion. Then there will be no more separation or sorrow, for verily, when Light finds his mate Dark, she will be swallowed up in his embrace.

The people may find the Forces which harmonize with them through the balanced method of concentration. The law of attraction brings Forces of like nature together, but the children themselves must know when to join their Forces. This becomes a simple matter when intuition is developed through the practice of concentration on the navel, which is the center of life, and the polarization of the spiritual and physical Forces issues from its position.

This ancient method of concentration will show the mates in physical forms where the Forces which will balance them may be found and to what degree of expansion they themselves vibrate. Then their unions will not be fraught with sadness, and the angels will cry aloud that the children of the King are coming home, and the sorrowing Earth will redeem its past.

I, Sano Tarot, have spoken.

6. JOINING THE FORCES
ON THE ROYAL ROAD TO PEACE

Hear me, Sano Tarot:

The joining of the harmonious Forces on the Earth planet balances the physical side of life with the spiritual side. Timekeeper, tell the people how to join their physical and spiritual Forces.

Hear me, the Timekeeper:

I say that the physical and spiritual Forces should be perfectly balanced. The service of the King can begin only when this is the case. Issue the order that the people find their own Force that they may also find the Forces which balance them. Vie with concentration to find their own planes of expression in their own realms of being. Each Force has a mate, which is the spiritual or physical side of itself. Finding the right mate in the right realm of being is the only method of returning to the King's realm of harmony. Joining the right Forces in the right realms of being gives the King's seal of approval on their union.

Hear me, the Timekeeper:

Harmony is found only when the balance of the physical and spiritual is perfect.

The Force of Mind should mate the Force of Heart only when the right planes of expression balance themselves.

The Force of Faith should mate the Force of Inspiration only on the right planes of expression.

The Force of Universal Love mates only the Queens of Heart.

The Force of Material Wealth gives itself through expansion. Its physical and spiritual sides are joined, and it serves the King in its own realm of being with harmony in its expression on Earth.

The Forces may all mate each other through observing the law of polarization. Vie with yourselves to listen intuitively for the call of the other half of yourself.

The Timekeeper has spoken.

I, Sano Tarot, say that the Timekeeper's advice is good.

Timekeeper, tell the story of singing mates on the planet Earth.

Singing mates are halves of Forces which must work together before perfection can be. Singing mates weld the Forces which combine for the joining of the physical and spiritual sides of life. The spiritual Forces mate the physical Forces and complete the circle of magnetic balance, which is the only hope of new life on the planet Earth. Joining the physical with the spiritual gives the answer to the prayer of the children of the King that they shall return to his kingdom of harmony.

Mate the right Forces on the right planes of expression, and the King can speak through the perfect channels thus made.

The Forces mated on the right planes of their expression make the electric balance through which may be given the peace which passes understanding and save the people of Earth from disintegration.

The Timekeeper has spoken.

Hear me, Sano Tarot:

I say that the Timekeeper has spoken truth.

Timekeeper, tell the people about the place of Seer's abode.

Saint Sano Tarot, I, the Timekeeper, will read from my record of time. In the place of Seer's abode, which is the realm of balanced Forces, only those who have attained the high, swift vibratory motion of balanced Forces can dwell. Understanding of natural Law and the overcoming of the flesh are the requirements of the Seers for those who would enter there. By the overcoming of the flesh, Seers are made.

The overcoming of the flesh is the highest test of the disciple on the road to peace.

Life, as expressed in the realm of Earth, is the result of the physical Forces balancing the spiritual Forces in the right realms of their being.

Hear the Timekeeper, who has spoken truth!

From the heights of spiritual expansion, the Seers guide the progress of the race submerged in the dense matter of Earth. Much that is difficult to understand by the people is under the right royal order of the Seers. On the heights of spiritual expansion, the will of the King is the Law.

Hear the Timekeeper!
Many things, which seem impossible to explain, become quite simple when the people think deeply about them. When they use their power of thought, their vibratory movement is quickened, and they are lifted into higher realms, thus joining the spiritual thought with the physical brain under the Law of the King that the spiritual and physical must be joined ere the law of expansion can express.

Mate the right Forces on the right planes of development in their right realms of being, and Life issues the order that it shall be done.

I, the Timekeeper, have spoken.

I, Sano Tarot, say that the Timekeeper speaks truth. The Seers know the law of vibration and recognize it as the only spiritual law.

Will is the masculine force of the planet Earth. Join it to the feminine force of receptivity on the right planes of expression and life issues the order of creation.

I, the Timekeeper, say that in the place of Seer's abode, Light is there and no Dark.

The Timekeeper speaks truth.
Light is the song of the Spirit. Dark exists only where Spirit is not. Issue the order that Spirit come and balance the physical forces of Earth, and there will be no more night. Timekeeper, tell the people of one day to come.

I, Sano Tarot, have spoken.

I, the Timekeeper, say that on the day when the King's children return to his kingdom of harmony, there will blaze a light so great that the Sun will fade.

I, the Timekeeper, say this, which is truth.

Light is the mate of Dark on the planet Earth, but the mates will be joined on their own planes in the Seer's abode, and Dark will issue the order of no more separation from her mate, Light, and right royally will they work together on their own plane. Dark will vie with Light, issuing the order that she, too, shine on the planet.

The day will come when the children of the King will hear his voice and obey his will.

I, Sano Tarot, have spoken.

Light joins his force to Dark because he must have a physical vehicle through which to express on the planet Earth. Joining his force to Dark gives him the right plane through which to express in the realm of Earth. Only balanced Forces can reproduce the King's ideal. Light gives spiritual force to the planet Earth. Therefore Light should tell the story of himself.

The Timekeeper has spoken.

I, Light, will speak.

When the Forces hurled themselves from the sphere of harmony, I, myself, attempted to bring them back, but they would not return, preferring the pain of unbalanced Forces to obedience to the King's Law. I saw that my only hope of saving them was to lower my swift motion and dwell with them until I could carry them home. So I used the negative realm Moon as my medium. Her spirit had gone astray with the mad Forces, but her physical elements still held her form. She gave herself to me and thus placed me in the right vibration to send myself into the dark realm of Earth, where the Forces had elected to dwell, and give them the light of the spirit of the King, in spite of themselves.

Having found a channel of balance through which I could express, I emerged from the heart of the Sun in seven great rays, each ray being pledged to find a medium in one of the seven realms of being, that I might quicken it with my fire. Through my magnetic rays, I joined myself to these mediums of electric nature, and at the point of contact, a center of light appeared. From these centers of balanced Forces, the King carries on his scheme of expanding and balancing the scattered Forces in the realm of Earth, thus saving his rebellious children and making them perfect expressions of all the life Forces and so bringing his kingdom of harmony into the realm of Earth.

I, Light, have spoken.

Light has spoken truth. By my order, he will tell the story of the planet mediums. The only hope of saving the dark planet Earth from disintegration was through the mediums which Light made.

I, Sano Tarot, have spoken.

I, Light, say that the centers of light called *planets* are the focussing points where I, being positive, have fused myself with the negative poles of the great primal Forces. Through my action on them, their essence is sent forth. These seven essences balance themselves in the lowered vibratory movement of Earth. Here their expansion and fusion, one with the other, is brought about.

    I fuse myself with the negative poles of the primal Forces that I may have balanced channels through which I can pour the light of the spirit of the King even to the lowest vibration of Earth.

    The planet Uranus hears my voice on the third degree of the vibratory law on the cycle of Gano Tarot, the Force of Universal Love. Hence the Force produced by the union of Light and Gano Tarot Saint's vibration is one of high spirituality.

    The planet Neptune hears my voice on the Seer's Insignia degree of Rano Tarot. From the union of Light and the Rano Tarot Seer's Insignia vibration, the Force of Faith is created on the planet Earth.

    The planet Venus hears my voice on the Seer's Insignia degree of Sano Tarot. From the union of Light and the Sano Tarot Seer's Insignia vibration comes the Force of Inspiration.

The planet Mars hears my voice on the Saint's degree of Tano Tarot. From the union of Light and the Tano Tarot Saint's vibration comes the Force of Material Wealth.

The planet Jupiter hears my voice on the Seer's Insignia degree of Fano Tarot. From the union of Light and the Fano Tarot Seer's Insignia vibration comes the Force of Heart.

The planet Mercury hears my voice on the Seer's Insignia degree of Pano Tarot. From the union of Light and Pano Tarot Seer's Insignia vibration comes the Force of Spiritual Mind.

The planet Saturn hears my voice on the Saint's degree of Ono Tarot. From the union of Light and Ono Tarot Saint's vibration comes the Force of Hope.

This is the story of the electric mediums through which I, Light, have spread the spirit of the King through the universe.[5]

---

[5] Do not think of the Sun and the planets as being apart from the Earth. Take an orange as an illustration of the Solar System. The outer skin of the orange represents the Sun. The white inner skin represents the Moon. The pulp is Jupiter and the juice is Venus. The bitter oil is Neptune and the red color is Mars. Mercury is represented by the tertiary period, which matures the fruit. Uranus is its vital energy. Saturn is represented by the seed and the Earth by the germ within the seed, which can reproduce itself only in lowered vibratory movement. So we call the lowest vibration in the Solar System, the *Earth*. The Solar System is well represented by an orange, and the same system exists in every living thing. In the orange, the planets fuse themselves in the Sun center or navel of the orange, just beneath the skin where the stem — which may be likened to the umbilical cord that pours life into the fruit — joins the form. From this center, the planets spread their essences through the form of the orange, each making a center for its given expression, which functions in its given manner as an integral part of the combination of forces called an *Orange*. Just so, the radiant centers which the people see with material vision and call *planets* are the points of contact where the magnetic rays of the Sun balance themselves with the electric life Forces, combinations of which make the many forms visible on Earth.

Sano Tarot.
When Light descended into a lower vibratory motion, he formed ten luminaries by fusing himself with ten negative forces. By the crossing and recrossing of the rays from these balanced centers of Light, man takes form, endowed with ten powers, which, when in full, conscious

Mates are always of opposite sex. I, Light, say that mates are always of opposite sex. The masculine Forces of the universe call to the feminine Forces, and the feminine Forces hear the call of their mates. When they find each other and their union is complete, then the sex force issues its order of new growth on the planet Earth. When the mates unite the spiritual and physical sides of themselves, they hear the call of balance, and strength to expand themselves into images of the King comes to them and makes them gods indeed.

I, Light, have spoken.

Timekeeper, tell the people about the overcoming of the flesh, which makes Seers of men.

Sano Tarot has spoken.

Right royal Sano Tarot, I, the Timekeeper, say that the overcoming of the flesh is the highest test of the disciple on the road to perfection on the planet Earth. Overcoming of the flesh means sin or unbalanced Force outgrown through understanding of the law of balance in the realm of the disciple's development. The spiritual day overcomes the physical night, and there is light on the subject of sin. The joining of the Forces on their own planes of development dispels the misunderstanding of life and the death of themselves.

The Timekeeper has spoken.

I, Sano Tarot, say that the Timekeeper speaks truth.

---

operation will make him a god indeed. Man is a spiritual being operating in a physical field where he is conscious only of five of the powers which enable him to live in an objective world. As he develops, he becomes aware of the spiritual poles of the powers he knows in the physical world, dormant within him, awaiting that day when he himself will bring them into full recognition and action. The appearance of new planets in the heavens measures the expansion of the consciousness of man. These planets have not been newly created when discovered. They have been hidden from man because of his low vibration, which, of necessity, limits his vision. When a new planet becomes visible to man, a corresponding one is quickened in his body and a new power expands in his life.

Serapis.

7. THE JOINING OF THE SEXES ON THE ROYAL ROAD TO PEACE ON THE PLANET EARTH

Hear me, Sano Tarot:

The joining of the sexes in the realm of Earth issues the order of the peace which passes understanding. The sexes are but halves of themselves. In the realm of harmony, the sexes were not separated, but in the realm of Earth, they are far apart and seek incessantly for each other, that they may find the completion of their scattered Forces.

In the realm of harmony, the sexes were joined in their own realms of being. Light dwelt with Dark, and there was light in the realm of harmony such as the Earth realm has never known. Heat mated cold. Cold gave herself to heat, and the atmosphere in the realm of harmony was good to feel. Love mated Hope on the right plane of their expression, and together they gave of the spirit of the King to the harmony realm. Faith mated Inspiration, and Inspiration gave herself to Faith, and Faith was sublime. Mind mated Heart on the right plane of their expression, and Heart gave herself to Mind, and loving-kindness dwelt in the realm of harmony.

After the separation, mates were lost to each other and could only mate the degrees on which they expressed. Light found a degree of Dark, but she knew him not. So Light wanders on in search of the full expression of Dark and her recognition of him, her mate. When their full reunion takes place, there will be no more night, for Dark will reign with Light, and Light will reign supreme.

I, Sano Tarot, have spoken.

Hear me, Sano Tarot:

I say that Light will reign supreme. Light will tell the story of himself when he shall have found his mate, Dark.

I, Light, mated Dark in the realm of harmony. I lost her in the upheaval when the Forces fell from their spiritual estate. I have searched through the ages for Dark, my mate. I have found her scattered degrees mated with inharmonious Forces and killing her spirit in the mismating. The spiritual side of life must balance the physical side before the mates can find completion.

When I, Light, have found the full expression of Dark, my mate, we will lose ourselves one within the other, and perfect balance will be our reward. When the spiritual and physical Forces are balanced, peace settles like a dove upon them, and the glory of the King shines about them.

I, Light, have spoken.

The seven realms of being hear only the call of their own realms. The seven degrees of each realm call to the realm which is their own and to the degrees of opposite sex in other planes of expression. The planes of expression answer the call of their opposites in all the seven realms of being. The Forces should fuse themselves only in the same realm of being, on opposite planes of expression in their own realms.

Hear me, Sano Tarot:

I say that the Forces should fuse themselves only on opposite degrees of their expression. Mate the masculine degrees with the feminine degrees, and the race has been served. Mate the feminine degrees with the feminine degrees, and death and destruction are the result. The great realms of being call their people so strongly that there is little danger of mismating with them. Joining the right degrees of expression is where the disciple must issue his own order with concentration to show him which Forces to join for his own growth and expansion. Answer your own prayer and vie with yourself to become conscious of your own realm of being, and you have found the royal road to peace. Tarot is the truth of the gods, long hidden from the knowledge of man because of his lack of desire for light on the subject of natural law and the veil that

Free Will let fall over his inner vision. Joining the Forces through willing them to unite darkens the spirit of the mates.

Light can find Dark in full completion only after he has fused himself with all her scattered degrees. Mates express in cycles of seven degrees, and each degree must find its balance before complete polarization is accomplished. Light must mate Dark only on the right degrees of expression through the union of his masculine degrees with her feminine degrees. Light should seek no other mate save Dark, and he should make the full cycle of his expansion through the cycle of hers, and together they will enter the kingdom of harmony.

I, Sano Tarot, have spoken.

This is the end of the Seven Songs of Tarot. I beseech you, my people, to give deep, intuitive attention to the truth contained herein. I know it is difficult to comprehend, but it is my desire that you strive to feel its meaning. As you meditate upon this exposition of vibratory law, the light of the ages will dawn within you, and nothing of truth will be hidden from you. It is through the balanced channel of intuition that the gods will clear away the veil of doubt and pour the light of understanding into your consciousness.

I, Sano Tarot, who govern the fourth or
Inspirational realm of being, say this, which is truth.

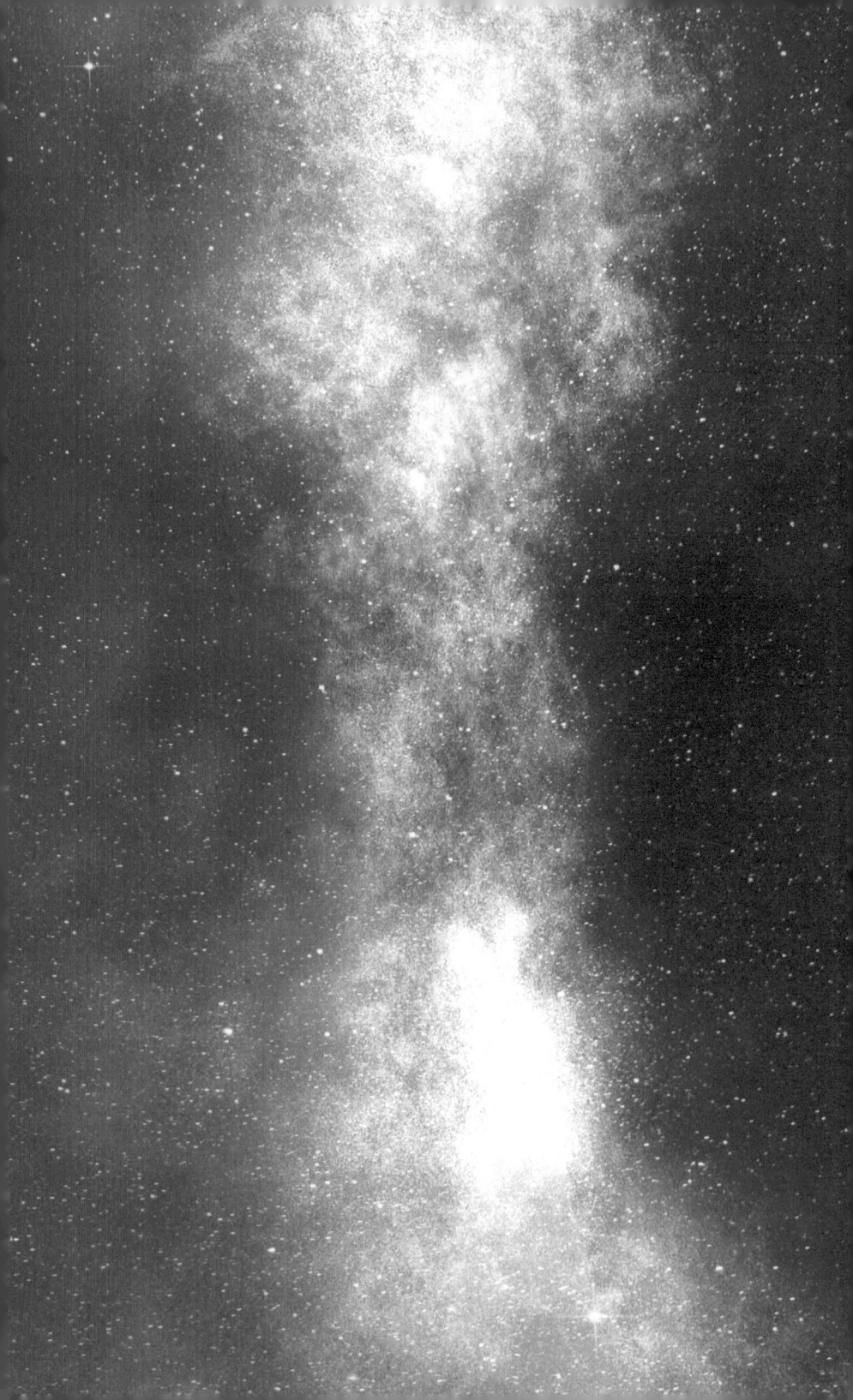

Book Two

THE SONG OF THE TIMEKEEPER

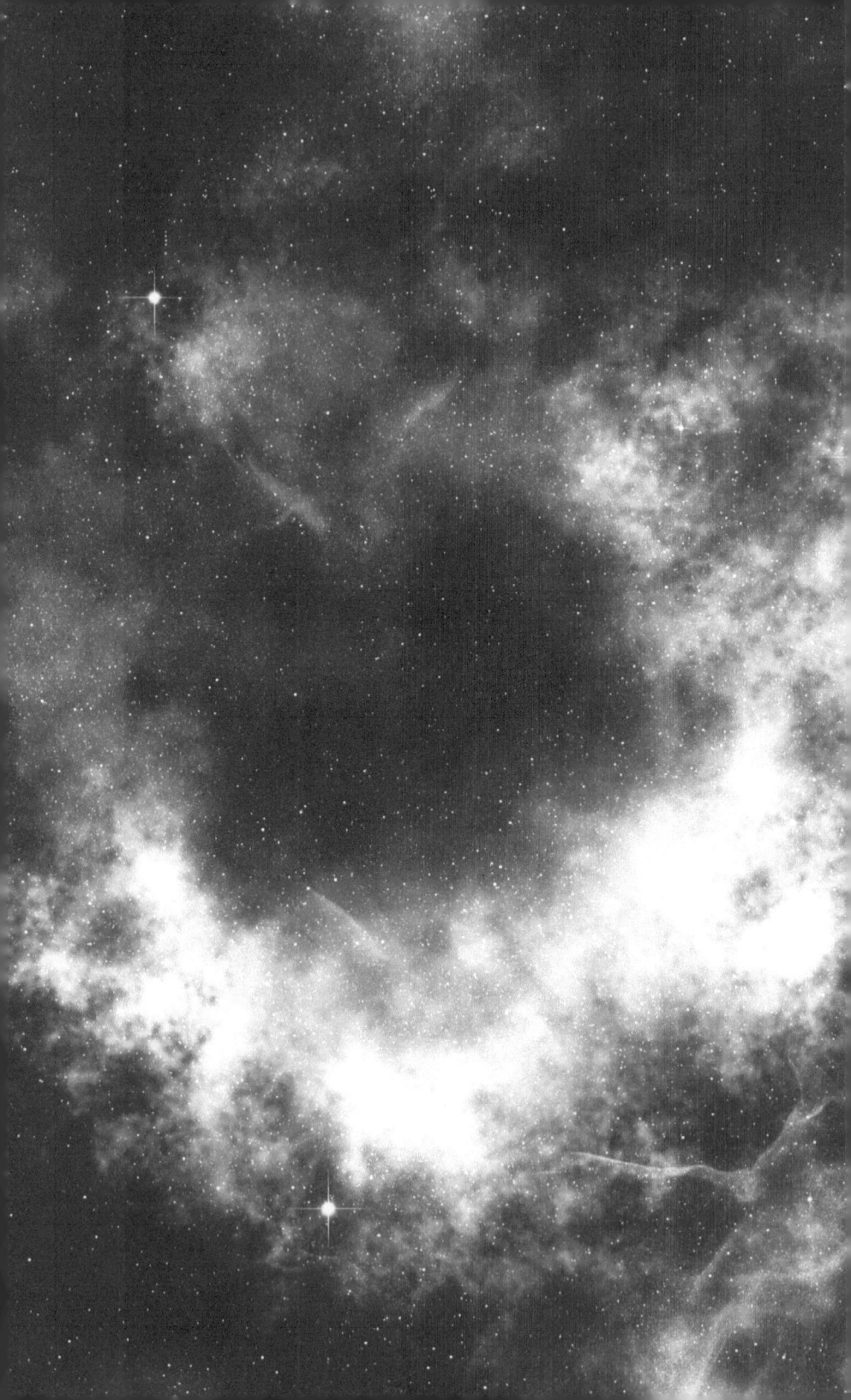

THE PEOPLE'S HOPE OF HAPPINESS IN THE REALM OF EARTH

Hear the Timekeeper!
Sano Tarot has spoken.

Most gracious High Priest Sano Tarot, I, the Timekeeper, will read from my Book of Time the record of Earth after the seven primal Forces fell from the sphere of harmony in the realm of Venus. I beg that you, most gracious sir, first tell the people about the sphere of harmony in which the Forces dwelt before they broke the law of their being and were driven out to learn the lesson of life through experience.

The Timekeeper's request will be granted by me.
Sano Tarot.

Once in the realm of Venus, there dwelt a King and his seven sons. Each son ruled a realm of his own, and each realm obeyed the will of its ruler. Pano Tarot ruled the realm of Mind. Fano Tarot ruled the realm of Heart. Tano Tarot ruled the realm of Material Wealth. I, Sano Tarot, ruled the realm of Inspiration. Rano Tarot ruled the realm of Faith. Gano Tarot ruled the realm of Universal Love, and Ono Tarot ruled the realm of Hope.

The seven sons of the King knew nothing of the kingdoms of their brothers, and each being unaware of anything not their own, harmony prevailed.

The King watched the kingdoms of his seven sons and was well pleased with the harmony expressed in their growth. When his sons reported to him that they wished new growth, he promised to give them new power to expand and thus continue to develop in harmony in their own realms. The new power he gave them was called *Free Will*. He gave each kingdom the right to use it for its own growth. He reminded them that the law of harmony must be respected, for though their strength be that of giants, a departure from harmony, which is the law of growth, would strip them of their strength and destroy their only hope of reaping the rich reward which comes only to those who grow in harmony.

All you who hear me speak, take heed! Your hope of happiness depends upon your harmony, and your harmony must issue itself from your own plane of development on your plane of expression in your own sphere of being. This is the law which issues the order of harmony in the universe.

Had the seven kingdoms of the seven sons of the King used the gift of the King for growth on their own planes alone, all would have been well. But they became mad with their new power when they knew that with it they could produce images in their own likeness. Not satisfied to reproduce themselves, they desired to produce other beings on other planes than their own, and discord and death overcame their realms, for the law of the universe decrees that growth can express only when the Forces of life develop on their own plane with the Forces which harmonize with them.

The King besought his sons to remonstrate with their people and command them to remain in their own realms and grow according to the law of creation, which is that each expression of life must expand on its own plane of development in its own sphere of being, and so fulfill the law.

But the kingdoms of the King's sons heeded not the words of their rulers, and discord issued itself through their realms. When the King knew that discord ran riot in the seven kingdoms of his sons, he hurled them out of the kingdom of harmony to prove for themselves that harmony is the law of growth, and only when they learned this and were willing to express on their own planes, could they return to their own kingdoms of harmony.

The seven kingdoms were scattered and mixed until there seemed no hope of ever separating them. Only degrees of them have been found by their rulers since they drew together in a whirling mass of inharmonious parts of themselves. The King called the great discordant sphere the *Earth*.

In the upheaval, the kingdom of Material Wealth remained intact, and although it was caught in the chaos of separation, it did not lose its balance, and because of its strength, it tied the scattered Forces with its material power. And through the eons, the kingdom of Material Wealth has expanded through the contact of the kingdoms of its brothers, for which they should be thankful, for not only does it give them a base to which to cling, but it has driven them on in their seeking to perfect themselves, even though they were under the impression that they were seeking Material Wealth for itself alone, which more than often was not true. What the people are really seeking is the perfection of themselves.

So, also, was the kingdom of Hope drawn into the vortex of separated Forces with its essence intact. Hope being a spiritual Force, it became the leaven in the lives of the people, and when Hope touches the problems which vex them, they never fail to make new effort to solve them. The great primal Forces, Material Wealth and Hope, being of opposite sex and complete in themselves, fused their Forces under the order of the King and thus made a center of balanced Forces in the midst of chaos. This center is the main dependence of all the scattered Forces, which, having no balance of their own, hold fast to what balance they can find with their feeble strength. You understand that five primal Forces were separated into infinitesimal particles of themselves, each particle restlessly seeking Forces needed to balance the Force already theirs. Hope and Material Wealth have given freely of themselves to the chaotic kingdoms of their brothers, giving each kingdom a center of balanced Forces that their subjects might ultimately find their own balance and expand their Forces in harmony. So the law of balance prevails in the lesser cycles of life as in the greater.

The seven kingdoms were mixed until there seemed no hope of ever separating them. Only degrees of them have ever been found by their rulers since they drew together in a whirling mass of inharmonious parts of themselves. The King called the great discordant sphere the *Earth*. Now the Timekeeper, who was ordained to keep a record of the movements of the new world, and to report faithfully to the King the progress made in the awakening of the seven realms of his seven sons, will go on with the story. Timekeeper, proceed.

Sano Tarot.

Hear me, the Timekeeper:

When the planet Earth was formed by the whirling discordant Forces of the seven kingdoms of the seven sons of the King, the King called me into being and ordered me to keep a record of those Forces which gave promise of realization of what they had done. This command I have faithfully obeyed and will now read from the Book I have kept since I, Time, was called by the King. Sano Tarot, who governs the fourth or Inspirational realm of being, only, may give the order under which I speak.

Only those who have awakened to a sense of the separation of their Forces can comprehend the meaning of my words, and to those alone do I speak.

Five primal Forces were scattered into infinitesimal particles of themselves when the planet Earth was born, and there seemed no hope of ever joining the right degrees of the right Forces together again. My work has been to guide them into channels which would draw these separated particles of primal Forces together by magnetic and electric action, that they might fuse themselves and so become stronger and more perfect in their polarization. Thus I, the Timekeeper, have served the King.

In the beginning, the realms of the seven sons of the King seemed one realm, so closely were they fused by Free Will, who elected himself king of the new planet Earth. The people may see that my work has not been simple. Now that they are awakening to the fact that they themselves may reach out and find the parts which they discarded long, long ago, my work is nothing like so difficult.

At first, the way seemed well-nigh hopeless. Then when the King's sons began to question as to the reason for the pain and suffering in the lives of their people, I, the Timekeeper, whispered to them that they were only parts of themselves and had not sufficient strength to make their lives harmonious. Free Will laughed at me, and I left them alone to find for themselves that I was speaking truth. So through the ages, the seven kingdoms of the seven sons of the King have suffered and questioned as to why life seemed so hard to comprehend.

Now they are, without doubt, becoming aware of their separation from the Forces which are needed to make perfect the whole of themselves. And I, the Timekeeper, am whispering again to the seven sons of the King that which they would not heed before, that all that matters with their people is that they are incomplete and need to balance their separated Forces and to become whole again and experience the harmony of well-rounded lives.

Believe the Timekeeper, who speaks truth! Nothing that the people do in the seven realms of the seven sons of the King will issue the order of harmony until they polarize the separated parts of themselves which were lost in the time of their hurling from the realm of Venus and crystalizing into a group of discordant particles of primal Forces which knew not what had happened to them.

Sano Tarot has spoken.

When I, the Timekeeper, began to record the reading of their lives, they were whirling in chaos, each ignorant of what had caused the upheaval and why they suffered so, for such small degrees of great kingdoms had no power to realize why the King had driven them out. Free Will, with utter disregard for the law of harmony, bade them come close together and fuse themselves, telling them that somewhere in the mass were their separated parts, each seeking for the other.

Hear me, the Timekeeper:
Mating the positive and negative Forces of life in harmony issues the order of expansion in the realm of Earth.

Hear the Timekeeper, who speaks truth! New life can spring only from the polarization of the positive and negative Forces.

When the positive Forces unite, discord and death ensue. So also, from the mating of two negative Forces come discord and ruin. Timekeeper, proceed.

Sano Tarot.

Gracious Sano Tarot, I beseech you to call Uriel into the echo and request him to tell his story of the King's plan to save the rebellious Forces.

The Timekeeper's request will be granted by me. Speak, Uriel!

Sano Tarot.

Good people of the realm of Earth, I, Uriel, greet you on this evening of grace. I invite you into my realm of White Fire and beg that you give me your undivided attention while I tell you a story which it is difficult for aught but alchemists to comprehend.

When the gods, under the order of the King, attempted to fuse the seven primal Forces into a sphere of balanced Forces, the experiment failed, in that the Forces took control of their own motion and madness beset them. So vital were they that they heeded not the command to obey the law of harmony in the fusion of their Forces, and as harmony is the one law of being, they became lost in chaos when promiscuity became their rule. The gods were sad indeed, for well they knew that these elemental children of the King would destroy themselves, and the work which had consumed countless ages would have to be begun all over again. So they held a council, and the master alchemists of the King's domain announced that there was only one hope of saving the situation. To be sure, the method which must be employed would cause the Forces great suffering, for the law has decreed that when harmony is not regarded, pain results.

The plan which was decided upon in the council of the gods was this: First, the vibratory motion of the mad Forces must be lowered, or slowed, if you will, so that they would find themselves in what seemed narrow confines and limitations, because of their slow movement. When the gods succeeded in bringing them to the lowest vibratory movement possible, they had them well in hand. Bear in mind that these elemental children of the King were imbued with Free Will and power of reproduction, so it was a delicate matter to hold them in their right relation to each other. Sad to relate, they knew only lust, which caused them unrest and disintegration. Love was among them, but they knew him not because of their lack of balance. Without Love, there can be no cohesion. So he who is nameless, though he has been called by various names, each of which is a symbol of the essence of life, which the gods call *White Fire* and the people call *Love*, volunteered to give his essence, which is Love, to save the mad Forces from destroying themselves. To accomplish this, he spread his essence over and through the dark mass, thus shedding his blood to save them. The alchemy of the gods is profound indeed.

Imagery is the wisest method in which to proceed. I place for your consideration a sphere of dark color whirling in the ether. The sphere was composed of seven elemental Forces, separated one from the other. Now Love was in their midst, but only through their harmonious fusion with each other could they become conscious of Love. Love, who brings Hope as his handmaiden, is always conscious of himself, so you sense the truth that Love offered himself as a conscious sacrifice to save the mad Forces. Ere this sacrifice could be completed, Love, whose vibration is high and swift, must lower his own movement and fuse himself with the negative Forces whirling in chaos, suffering with them the pain of limitation, and lying with them in the grave of dense matter until they were quickened by his Fire, receiving thereby an impulse which will drive them on to perfection.

The days of creation are of great length. Three days passed ere Love's seed was planted in the very heart of the Earth. Then, trembling with ecstasy, Love cried: "It is finished!" And the motion of the planet Earth was quickened and Earth shone with dawning light, and Love rejoiced.

Be not dismayed at the lack of understanding of the people. I speak truth when I say that when it was known that Love had volunteered to lower his swift motion that the rebellious children might be saved, I, Uriel, volunteered to become the body of Love, the great unifying or cohesive principle of the universe. Only thus could Love's swift motion contact the discordant Forces and, through the crossing of them with his essence, bring about their transmutation by quickening their movement. So, clothed with Love's fire, I fell like a burning fagot into chaos, pledged to remain Love's channel of expression until he brought his sacrifice to completion and the seven primal Forces were saved in spite of themselves.

Love's burial in matter has been the keynote of all religions, which have stirred the spirit of the people of Earth. And the profound belief, though often unconscious, in the resurrection of matter through Love, has kept Hope alive within them, and when Hope lives within the people, the gods are assured that they will seek understanding and find it. *Adieu.*[6]

I, Uriel, have spoken.

Uriel has told his story well. Timekeeper, proceed.

Sano Tarot.

When the years began to be counted by me through the mating of the seasons, the fierce whirling had become slower, and moisture appeared from the mating of the positive force of the Sun and the negative force of the Moon. Saint Sano Tarot, kindly allow Jehovah, god of the Moon, to tell the story of the love song of Sun and Moon.

I will grant your request, Timekeeper. Speak, Jehovah, god of the Moon.

Gracious Sano Tarot, I obey your will. When the separated Forces fell into chaos, I was appointed to assist the gods, whose work it was to balance the positive and negative poles of these Forces and so give them form in their own realms, that life might progress. My work consisted of gathering together the negative degree of the

---
[6] *Adieu (French)* — goodbye.

scattered Forces, which had held fast to harmony in the upheaval, that the King, who had made the Sun for his dwelling place, might have a balance pole through which to express. I sent Gabriel, my messenger, through the realm of Earth, and he found many negative degrees of the great primal Forces singing a minor song in their loneliness, having refused to obey the order of Free Will that they mate regardless of harmony. They obeyed my order that they come close together. My knowledge of the positive nature of the Sun made plain to me his need of negative balance. You can readily see that without a negative balance, die positive force of the Sun would have had the almost hopeless task of fusing himself with each negative degree whirling in the ether. And thus a much longer period of time would have been required for the scattered Forces to have reached their present polarization and expansion.

The degrees of negative nature which I drew close together were of such strength that they defied the command of Free Will that their fusion take place without regard to the law of polarization. This law has decreed that only harmonious degrees of harmonious Forces may fuse themselves and feel growth and expansion in their new expression.

You comprehend that negative Forces express generation rather than creation, so it has been said that the spirit, which is positive and creative, had fled from the Moon, leaving her cold and dead, which is to say that there is no positive element in the Moon. I held her like a great quivering womb in the midst of the chaotic Forces, awaiting the Timekeeper's call for her mating with the Sun. This time came when the Sun drew near enough to the whirling discordant sphere to feel the attraction which harmonious opposites always feel. Through the ether, the love song of Moon hummed its way straight into the fire center of Sun, and he drew her out of the chaotic realm of separated Forces and listened while she told her story to him.

When he heard that from the beginning, she had felt his need of negative balance and had grown strong with longing to serve him, he bade her call Free Will to witness that she had never disregarded the law of harmony, but had awaited the coming of her lord, the Sun. Free Will corroborated her story and bade her go out from the whirling mass of discordant Forces, and the Moon fell away from his kingdom. The Sun caught her and held her for his own, and on the day of their union, moisture appeared on the planet Earth, and growth in all forms of life went forward in increased measure. This is the story of the love song of Sun and Moon, though it has been expressed in less detail in the revelation given by the right royal Sano Tarot, I, Jehovah, god of the Moon, have spoken.

I place my seal of truth on the words of Moon god Jehovah. So great a part has he played in the formation of the world that he has frequently been confused in the minds of the people with the nameless One. Hear the Timekeeper again!

I, Sano Tarot, have spoken.

Most gracious Sano Tarot, I wish to tell the people about the forces which have been called *Adam* and *Eve*, by your leave.

Hear the Timekeeper! He will speak to the people of Earth under the order of Sano Tarot, who gives his consent that he tell them of the forces called Adam and Eve.

When the Forces dwelt in harmony, there was no separation of their positive and negative sides. They dwelt together, and harmony reigned supreme. Then the positive and negative Forces became separated. This is the sad day of which I am speaking, for never has the negative pole called Eve returned to the realm of harmony with the other half of herself called Adam. Since then, she has been seeking him, and he has been seeking her, but they have found each other only in degree, mated to Forces not in harmony with them, and in so doing, dying the death which follows the mismating of the life Forces.

The Garden of Eden was a realm of balanced Forces. Perfect order was there, and harmony prevailed. Saint Sano Tarot, I beseech you to tell the people of the harmony which existed in the Garden of Eden. Your way of singing the harmony song is over and above anything of its kind which the people have ever heard on the subject of harmony. Pray begin, most gracious sir.

Hear me, Sano Tarot:
   I will grant the request of the Timekeeper and tell the people of the harmony in the Garden of Eden.
   Listen when the rain falls on the grass, and you will hear the soft humming of myriad tiny notes, which sing only their own song, so they sing the harmony song of their own realm, which issues the order of rain in the realm of Earth. Then listen again to the rays of sunlight whispering their own sweet tones in the air. Hear in the evening time the dark shadows making their own weird sounds, and the rising Sun making merry with its song of light, and the ocean, beating on the sand, giving its own dull sound with its own breaking waves on its own shore. So in all nature, each song issues the order of harmony through its own realm in the universe.
   Now Timekeeper, proceed with your story of the forces called Adam and Eve.

Sano Tarot has spoken.

I, the Timekeeper, thank the right royal High Priest, Saint Sano Tarot, for his illustration of the harmonious vibrations when they sing their own song in their own realm of being. I return to my story of the forces called Adam and Eve. To be sure, I had not been called into being when the Forces dwelt together in harmony in the Garden of Eden, but Light, who was there, told me that Free Will, who caused the upheaval in the realm of Venus, could not at first draw the negative force called Eve away from the positive force called Adam. So he entered the Garden as Wisdom and whispered to the negative force called Eve, that if she would come away from her positive half, that he, Wisdom, would increase her knowledge seven times. But if she remained a part of the positive force called Adam, her power would wither and die.

When the negative force called Eve heard the voice of Wisdom, she knew that the law of life demanded that she grow or disintegrate. Then she withdrew from her positive side and began her search for knowledge through experience. When she found herself alone, she forgot the law of the King, that the spiritual Forces must be balanced with the physical forces and that only forces of like nature fused on the right degrees of their expression can know expansion and harmonious creation; and within her Free Will became lust and set himself up as King of this realm, created by the negative force called Eve through her mistaken use of the divine gift of Free Will.

The positive force called Adam became aware that his negative side had left him, and he followed her voice, which became confused with other voices until he heard it clearly no more. Through the ages, he has listened, but the voice of Eve has ever eluded him. Eve too, searched blindly for him, both fearing to be alone, for the spirit of them knew that when the life Forces are not balanced, harmony cannot exist. Because of the lack of polarization of the positive and negative Forces, their vibratory movement was lowered, and the dense realm of Earth came into being. With this creation, I, Time, came into being. I found the positive force called Adam and the negative force called Eve still seeking unceasingly for each other. It has been my pleasure to present them with degrees of themselves, and the realm of Earth has gained great balance. And now, after countless ages, I see Hope glimmering through the separated positive Adams and negative Eves, whispering of the drawing near of the completion of their scattered Forces. Thus will the positive force called Adam take the negative force called Eve unto himself, and perfect balance will issue itself in the realm of Earth, and harmony will reign supreme.

This is the story of Adam and Eve as it really is. I beseech the people to believe me, the Timekeeper.

The Timekeeper has spoken truth. It will be plainly seen by those who have sufficient balance of Forces to have intuitive vision, that had the seven realms of the seven sons of the King used the gift of Free Will as directed by the King, they would have fused themselves and expanded, each partaking of the other in harmony. Thus they would have been saved from the long journey through friction and death caused by breaking the law of their being.

Sano Tarot.

I, the Timekeeper, say that the realm of Venus may be likened to the great subconscious realm of the universe, and it was here that the great experiment took place. When the positive and negative Forces of this realm became separated, they were scattered to the four winds and moved helplessly about, and they are still blindly seeking to polarize themselves. Give me your undivided attention. The primal gods, who are the seven sons of the King, were ordered by the King to bring their kingdoms back into harmony. They saw the scattered degrees of their kingdoms drifting apart and Free Will driving them away from the degrees, which were the ones needed to give them balance. I, the Timekeeper, was called to watch the doings of Free Will and ultimately outwit him and bring the right degrees of the Forces together again. So I have done, and many degrees of the Forces have balanced themselves. And others are strong enough to consciously seek new life, thereby discovering many degrees of Forces which might have drifted away from them until I, Time, brought them together again.

Of all the people of Earth, you will be surprised to learn that they are divided into only seven kinds. However, such is the truth, and — listen carefully now — expansion and harmony balance their lives; that is, the degrees of the Forces separated from them can find them only when they live the kind of life belonging to the kind of people they are, or according to which of the seven kingdoms they owe allegiance.

Hear the Timekeeper, who speaks truth!

Sano Tarot.

Most gracious sir, tell the people how to call to themselves the separated parts of themselves which must be joined before balance can issue its order in their lives. Make them understand that they themselves are the Forces, and according to the combinations of the primal Forces in their bodies, do they express in the realm of Earth.

Timekeeper, this is your part of the story, which I beg you to continue.

Sano Tarot.

Pardon my seeming reluctance to speak on this subject, most gracious sir, but the people have so stumbled and fallen on this very thing that I dread to be misunderstood. However, I know that they are more balanced now, and many will comprehend and see light glimmering through the subject of sex. When the people know that in the plan of creation sex union was a spiritual process, they will glimpse the depths to which they have fallen and the heights to which they may rise. It will require deep intuitive thought to realize the truth of my statement. But in this, the inception of a spiritual cycle of the expression of the life Forces, many of the children of the King, who have long been bound by fetters of their own forging, will emerge from the shadows into the sunlight of truth and know that through their spiritual will, which is the will of the King, they may call the degrees of the Forces needed to balance the cycle of their lives and with quickened vibratory movement they will know these degrees have expanded and polarized themselves in their bodies, bringing new life and regeneration. You see, sex is universal. Harmonious sex union is the law of growth. When two degrees of the positive and negative Forces unite in perfect polarization, growth ensues. When two degrees of the positive and negative Forces unite in inharmony, disintegration and death follow.

The law demands that all union of the sex Forces take place only when the right realms of being, vibrating on the right degrees of their development, call each other in terms unmistakable. There is a way to determine your realm of being and to know without doubt what degree of what Force you need to balance the Force already yours.

    The ancient Seers used the terrapin as a symbol of balanced Forces because the terrapin draws all its life Forces under one shell and so expresses its life in its own way, balancing its movements through intuition. So, as the terrapin bears the shape of the solar plexus, which is the negative or physical pole of the Forces centered in the navel plexus, the Seers used it as a symbol of balanced concentration. And they beseech the people to master this method of concentration, which develops intuition and makes clear their spiritual vision, without which they can only grope in the dark, which ignorance makes its own. Find the central cell of your body, and you have found the still place of balanced Forces.

The Timekeeper has spoken.

Hear the Timekeeper, all you seekers after truth! Be convinced of the wisdom of his words. Timekeeper, proceed.

Sano Tarot.

To find the realm of being which is your own, center your attention on your navel, which is the eye of the solar plexus. Desire deeply to understand where your place in the universe is and how to express harmony in that realm. In less time than seems possible, you will feel the call of your own realm of being and you will know whether you lack positive or negative force to balance your life's expression and issue the order of its harmony.

The Timekeeper has spoken.

I, Sano Tarot, beseech you to accept the advice of the Timekeeper and learn the Seer's method of balanced concentration, for only thus can you develop your channel of intuition, through which you may find your place in the universe and know how to balance your own Forces and join your harmony song with the music of the spheres.

Sano Tarot has spoken.

I, the Timekeeper, have told you that the people of Earth are divided into seven kinds, each kind belonging to one of the seven realms ruled by the seven sons of the King. The seven sons of the King were appointed gods of the realms they ruled when they became conscious of their responsibility, and each pledged himself to bring his subjects back into the kingdom of harmony, expanded to their full power of consciousness, and fused in harmony with the realms of their brothers.

When you find the center of balance in your body, ask the spirit of yourself to make plain to you the seven great primal Forces which make you what you are. You will find that the Force of Mind (Pano Tarot) calls its people with much learning as their way of growth. The Force of Heart (Fano Tarot) gives its development through the righting of the wrongs of the people. The Force of Material Wealth (Tano Tarot) expands by placing the thought on the Material Wealth of the universe. The Force of Inspiration (Sano Tarot) grows through inspiring the people to higher calling. Faith (Rano Tarot) makes progress through faith in the universe. Universal Love (Gano Tarot) expands by pouring out its fire and quickening the spirit of the people for the uplift of humanity. The Force of Hope (Ono Tarot) gives growth and peace to all who use it. Use your own Force as Light uses itself with abandon, trying to grow into a full expression of itself.

When you have learned which of the seven primal Forces is yours, lose no time in readjusting your thoughts and deeds to its note, as though you had been transplanted into a new way of living, and you will be surprised at how much easier the new way is. To be sure, you may not feel the perfect harmony you desire in your life's expression at first trial, but persist, and ere long, it will make itself felt in great measure.

With harmony expressing itself in your realm of being, you will be able to tell whether you are too positive or too negative and know the vibration which you now express in any given realm. Understand that the law of vibration changes your plane of expression according to your power of will and your expansion of consciousness. Certain acts bring like results, and when your action corresponds to the vibration you are expressing, then you are working on your own plane of expression in your own realm of being, and harmony of Forces will expand your consciousness and fill you with new life.

Hear the Timekeeper: he speaks truth!
Sano Tarot.

Right royal Sano Tarot, I thank you. This question of spiritual sex is not an easy one to handle.

None other could do it so well as you, Timekeeper.
Sano Tarot has spoken.

I will make the matter as plain as possible to the people who are just lifting their consciousness to spiritual heights and trust them to comprehend my meaning. When Eve drew away from Adam, then was all sex force separated. This was necessary for the expansion of both sexes. I will speak of why it was necessary so there will be no misunderstanding of the law of nature, which demands expansion or disintegration. When the great primal Forces had reached the limit of their expansion, they were forced into new growth to save them from disintegration. This, you can see, was a wise law without which there would have been no world and no people who are now growing into gods in that they have gathered balance of Forces which gives them new light and new strength with which to expand. The fall of the Forces into chaos was caused by their disobedience to the wise law of the King in the fusion of their Forces with no thought of polarization.

It may plainly be seen that since the positive and negative, or spiritual and physical Forces, were the only Forces used in the creation of the universe, they must be the same Forces which make the universe what it is today. This being the case, the separated Forces expressing in the realm of Earth must be of the same kind of stuff of which they were made. The whole perfect scheme of the King is working itself out through the balancing of the life Forces in the realm of Earth, which may be called the *great laboratory of life* where the scattered degrees of the seven primal Forces are expanding and balancing themselves, the result of which will be the kingdom of harmony on Earth.

You will readily see that every visible thing and every invisible thing, every thought and every mental image, the strata of soil and the currents of air, the sunlight and the shade, day and night, have sex. Even the moonlight sending its long shafts through the shadows is seeking the positive side of itself, which permeates the Earth through the action of the Sun, whereby it may issue the order of balance and new growth, thus balancing its own negative side.

Will you follow me on a journey by way of illustration? When the planet Earth was young, the seven gods, who are the seven sons of the King, held a council where the balancing of the separated positive and negative Forces was discussed. It was a delicate matter to undertake, for should the degrees of the separated Forces mistake the degrees which belonged to them and two degrees of antagonistic Forces unite, death and destruction would result. The gods knew that the only hope of saving the planet Earth and bringing about the expansion and fusion of the seven primal Forces was in the right balancing of the positive and negative degrees of these Forces, which were separated one from the other. So they spoke to the high priests who served them, issuing the order that the positive and negative degrees must seek each other diligently through the mass of chaos, and let nothing interfere with their seeking until they had gathered to themselves the degrees needed to balance the degrees already theirs, so that they might further assist in the final balancing of the great positive and negative poles of life which will result in the same perfect balance of the positive and negative Forces, which issued the order of harmony in the realm of Venus, expanded sevenfold. The high priests issued the order, but alas, the people misunderstood. They thought that the word *mating* meant only the physical sex union, which reproduced their kind. To be sure, this union is an important one in this physical world of unbalanced Forces, and the same law of balancing the right Forces prevails here as in the spiritual fusion of the Forces.

Do not misunderstand me, my children, as you misunderstood the high priests, for in the spiritual fusion of your Forces lies the making of harmony and life or discord and death. When the Forces were lost in the maze of separation, then was the time they should have sought with care their separated degrees of Forces. But in spite of the high priests' order, they mated without thought, driven by desire for physical sensation. Such fusion of Forces lowered the vibratory movement of themselves and brought into being the dense physical world, in which, filled with lust, many of the children of the King have killed their spirit and lost their hope of harmony. In all phases of sex union, the same law prevails. The mates must be of the same realm of being or the same primal Force, and they must express an opposite degree of vibration at the season of mating.

You must understand that being in a masculine body does not mean that you always express a masculine vibration, for many moments of expression of both sexes come on a vibration not indicated by their physical bodies. Thus you see the necessity for deep intuition before any sex union.

People contemplating physical marriage should use all their power of thought and intuition and determine, without doubt, that their selected mates are of the same great primal Force as they themselves. This being the case, they should use more thought and intuition before fusing their Forces for the purpose of physical reproduction, lest inharmony rings the bell of death on their union. The people will make progress in the development of their intuition when they learn to concentrate in the way taught by the gods, and there need not be so many dire mistakes in the marriages of the mortals of Earth. Through polarization of the life Forces, the people are lifted to a higher plane of vibration.

Now to return to the spiritual mating of the Forces, which is the burden of the Seers on the heights of spiritual expansion and the hope of the people for the peace which passes understanding in the realm of Earth.

When the forces were separated, I, the Timekeeper, saw them whirling apart. The degrees needed to fuse and balance themselves were running away from each other. And I knew there was nothing to do but wait until a sufficient number of positive and negative degrees had come together in harmony through the law of attraction and had formed a center of balance whereby the other chaotic degrees of the seven primal Forces could steady themselves, and I could bring together the right degrees of Forces to complete their balance.

The time is here when this spiritual fusion of the Forces may be accomplished through the deep spiritual desire of the awakened people, and I, the Timekeeper, will resume the work so long ago ordered by the seven gods of the seven life Forces.

It will not be a simple matter to make the people understand. But that I did not know that some of them will, I would turn from the task and leave them to continue to follow their own mistaken idea of mating. However, for the sake of the few, I will proceed.

The seven life Forces were scattered into seven parts of themselves, and these seven parts were again scattered into infinitesimal parts of themselves when the planet Earth was young, and I, the Timekeeper, was called into being. Such was the confusion that even the gods despaired of joining the right realms together, and the right degrees of each realm were certainly lost in the mass. But when I came into being and gave them my word to use every effort to bring the right realms together, they left the matter in my hands, and to this day, I, Time, am quietly bringing the right Forces together and making the way clear for the right degrees of the right Forces to find each other. Little do the people of Earth realize the part Time plays in the development of their lives.

As the eons passed, I have succeeded in balancing many of the separated degrees of the seven primal Forces so that the parts still drifting alone have come closer, and my work is nothing like so difficult. Believe me when I say that what has been accomplished in the great universe has also been accomplished in the lesser universe, man. There is a host of people who have attained balance of Forces in the lower vibratory realms and may now progress in higher, rarer realms. Their whole expression of life is being quickened, and spiritual vision or intuition is developing within them. These are they who have risen through the trials which beset unbalanced Forces, groping in dense matter into the light of spiritual understanding. These are the Seers who have overcome the flesh and now express the radiance of spirit. These are they who have earned the power to draw to themselves the Forces yet needed to make them complete expressions of all the life Forces by their spiritual will, which is the will of the King, in that there is no lust in it, only deep desire for expansion and balance of Forces. These spiritual degrees of the Forces come without a turning to those whose will is merged with the will of the King, and lo, like homing birds, they nest with their kind, giving new balance and more abundant life.

When the people understand that they are but parts of perfect Forces, they will seek without delay for their separated Forces, which will make them whole. When they find them, they will find balance, and where there is balance of Forces, harmony is also there.

The people are composed of degrees of Mind and degrees of Heart, Inspiration, Hope, Faith, Love, and Material Wealth. It may be difficult to comprehend that each degree of the life Forces has sex, and some of the people have positive degrees of Mind, and others have negative degrees of Heart. Some have no degree of Inspiration, while others have many degrees of Faith, and Love has been left out of many lives.

Through the ages, I, the Timekeeper, have fused many degrees of the Forces in their right relation as to their sex, that is, a positive and a negative degree belonging to one of the great primal Forces. The right royal Sano Tarot, who governs the fourth or Inspirational realm of being, has told you that the vibratory movement of Earth has been raised as the Forces have balanced themselves, and now many people are of such rare, swift vibratory nature that they may fuse their separated Forces through their spiritual Will. This story cannot be repeated too often, for unless the spiritual law is understood and observed, Earth will fall into deeper chaos and lose what balance it has attained.

When the people know, through their intuition, what degrees of what Forces they lack, they may concentrate in the balanced way and lift their spirit high in the ether, where they may command the degrees of vibration needed to complete their full expression of the life Forces to fuse themselves with the degrees already theirs. This is the gift of the gods to those who have overcome the flesh and who dwell in that rare state of consciousness known as the Over-Soul[7] plane of vibration.

For the sake of making the vibratory laws of practical use to the people, the gods have given names to the degrees of vibration which they have used throughout the ages in balancing the life Forces that they might work with Hope in lifting the Forces into a perfect world.

Ideals are generated by the harmonious fusion of the life Forces. And when the disciple has held an ideal long enough to assimilate it and get his bearings, as it were, in the new conception, he has changed his vibratory motion, so the gods have called the first degree of consciousness in a new vibration, the Rope Walker's degree. This is a masculine vibration, in that it creates a new conception.

The second plane of vibration in the expansion of the life Forces is called *Reader's degree*. Here the disciple realizes that creation is working through him and that he is expanding in consciousness. The Reader's degree is feminine in that it has received the new vibration of the Rope Walker. These two great vibrations have long ago fused themselves so perfectly that the gods have used their united forces to form a base in each of the great primal Forces. This base they have called the *Purple Order vibration* because it is balanced and creative. So in the fusion of the Forces which make balance in the realm of Earth, the Rope Walker and the Reader's vibrations are no longer counted as separated parts of Forces, for

---

[7] *Over-Soul* — the Universal Soul, also known as *Alaya* (*Sanskrit*, "abode"); the Father-Mother. All individual souls are its rays or sparks and are able to merge with it.

they have become one, to which the others cling in the balancing of their own scattered Forces.

So there now remain two positive and two negative realms of vibration in each of the great primal realms to find their balance before Earth issues the order of balanced Forces. The gods have called the two negative realms the *Saint's vibration* and the *vibration of Seer's Insignia*. All these vibrations express in the lives of the people as states of consciousness. When the disciple expresses the Saint's vibration, he realizes what its spiritual expansion means in his life. When he expresses the Seer's Insignia, he looks ahead into the future of this state of consciousness and sets his face toward that goal.

The first of the two positive vibrations is the Seers in Higher Vibration. Here the disciple seeks to widen his knowledge of vibratory Law. When his knowledge is complete, he has lifted his consciousness to the vibration of High Priest. Here he knows that he knows. He can look back over the vibratory path by which he has advanced and is prepared to enter the Over-Soul realm of consciousness.

Children of Earth, know you this: Before you can find your balance of Forces and with it your harmony, you must be certain which of the great primal Forces is your own. When the upheaval was in the realm of Venus, the seven primal Forces fell into chaos, and you were a spark from one of them; therefore, this spark is your individuality and a potential god. You have been told how to determine which realm is your own by balanced concentration, by which your intuition will be developed — and through this channel, you will know.

When complete expansion and balance issue its order in each of the seven kingdoms of the seven sons of the King, then balance will once more express in the Forces which form the planet Earth, and when the great positive side of life is fused with the great negative side, the result will be a universe of balanced Forces expanded seven times.

Although this may seem a long, long time away when we judge life by its present imperfection, compared with the eons which have passed, it is really quite near at hand.

Years make no impress on the heart of life, which through the ages, has driven the life Forces on toward perfection. When the people desired to advance in their consciousness of life and its law, I, the Timekeeper, have opened the way through which they have found light on the subject of their spiritual expansion. Thus has the great heart of the universe been beating and keeping aglow the fire on life's hearthstone, and thus have the gods brought harmony where discord was.

I, the Timekeeper, have spoken.

Hear me, Sano Tarot:

I say that during the eons of expanding and balancing the great life Forces, the vibratory movement of Earth has been steadily raised. Now its rate of vibration is becoming swifter with each cycle of twelve hours, and it will require balance of Forces on the part of the people to respond to its new movement. Therefore, I beseech you to heed what has been said to you again and again in this message from the Hermitage.

It is my hope that all the people will believe this basic truth, though this is too much to expect when they know nothing of life's law and order of expansion. I have told them what is essential to know, and if they have found a bit of illumination, they will seek and find more. I say to them that the seven life Forces find their highest expression of polarization in man. Every living thing expresses degrees of the seven primal Forces, and when the people have balanced these Forces within themselves, there will be no more of the ills which unbalanced Forces bring.

When you feel that your life's expression is incomplete, concentrate your Forces in the balanced way. Develop your intuition, then ask your spirit to show you to which of the great primal Forces you belong. Should you feel intuitively that your individual life spark came out from the Force of Mind, then know that you can find harmony only by using this Force in all that you do. This law must be your rule no matter how or where you are expressing in your progress toward completion. Thus we will suppose that you belong to the primal Force of Mind, and at a given time, you are developing within you a degree of the Force of Heart. Now you plainly see that you have two laws to obey to bring harmony into your life and your work. Mind is your basic Force, and you must make your expression of the Force of Heart obey this basic Force.

I will illustrate with a homely thought. A man whose life was sad and full of pain was sent to serve mankind, and while he lived, this was to be his work. But this man longed to master science, so he forgot where his place was and lost himself in the storing of his mind with learning. But he was not happy, though his vast learning brought other men of learning to his feet. He became restless and sought spiritual counsel. He was told that his place was to serve, and in no other way could he bring harmony to himself. Then the man saw the light; no matter where or what he was expressing, his work must be made to serve. "Just so," said his counselor, "You must use your own Force no matter what plane of vibration you are expressing at a given time."

In the language of vibration, this man belonged to Fano Tarot, the great Force of Heart, whose people must serve to grow. But he ignored his own realm of being and entered the realm of Pano Tarot, the Force of Mind, so he could find no joy or peace in his work until he used his own Force by making his learning serve the people. Then harmony entered his life, and the people blessed his name.

So you see that you must use your own basic Force as the director of any Forces you may be using for the time being to gain knowledge and polarization with the other primal Forces. When the primal Forces are polarized within you, there will be little danger of failure in the work you choose.

Attention, all you who would have harmony in your lives! Make no move until you are sure that your own primal Force may be used in the expression of life you are seeking, for if you cannot use your own Force, there will be no harmony and clear vision in what you do and where there is no harmony there can be no success.

Again I will illustrate so that your understanding may be clear. Here is a man who belongs to the great Force of Inspiration, and he longs to right the wrongs of the people, which is the work that belongs to the Heart Force. And none other may do the work which belongs to the people of the Heart Force and bring harmony into their undertaking, but even so, the man who belongs to the Force of Inspiration may serve the people by inspiring them to make new effort in all they do. Thus he will serve in his own way, and because he is using his own Force, he will serve the people with harmony and success.

Thus with all the great primal Forces which are scattered through every living thing, each must do its own work in its own way, in whatever position it finds itself, and only in so doing can harmony and growth issue their order in the expression of the life Forces. Perhaps when I say that square pegs cannot fit in round holes, you will understand how impossible it is for the people who belong to one primal Force to express their lives in the manner ordered for the people of other realms.

When your channel of intuition is perfected, you will know without doubt to which of the primal Forces you belong. Then I beseech you to use it and no other, so that harmony can issue its order in your lives. Timekeeper, speak again to the people.

I, Sano Tarot, have spoken.

Most gracious Sano Tarot, I, the Timekeeper, obey your command. When the scattered Forces first knew me, the world was young and ignorant of its possibilities. When I tried to tell the rebellious children of the King why they suffered so, they would not listen. So I bided my time, whispering here and there to those who would listen of why their lives were awry and how they might find harmony. Those who would not listen went stumbling on in their mistaken way, though life held out to them its own perfect solution of their problems. Ages have passed, and still, the children will not listen, but it gives me pleasure most profound that now a great host of them are awake and are seeking knowledge of life and its law. I have long watched them walking on the brink of destruction, and now I am filled with joy that so many of them have thrown away the blindfold of ignorance and are looking wisely and unafraid at life.

These rare people will comprehend the truth of my words. It is to them that light is given on the subject of sex from a spiritual and universal viewpoint, and they, having the light of balanced Forces within them, make music of knowledge in the realm of illumination. When the people understand the vibratory laws which govern the balancing of their Forces and know that vibrations are as real as if they could hold them in their hands and feel their weight, they will make no delay in mastering their action through balanced concentration. When they have learned the lesson of life through the balanced method of concentration, they will have raised their vibratory movement to the heights of spiritual expansion and will have earned the privilege of selecting the degrees of Forces which are needed to complete their lives and of commanding them through their spiritual will to fuse themselves in their bodies and bring them the harmony of balanced Forces.

The question of sex has ever been a stumbling block to the people of the dense physical world, who mistook lust for love and united their Forces with Forces not their own and fused their degrees of Forces with the wrong degrees of other Forces, thus destroying themselves and their mates by breaking the law of their being which has decreed that only mates of the same primal Force expressing opposite sex vibrations can fuse themselves with polarization as the result.

When you concentrate, find from the spiritual mind of yourself whether you are positive or negative in your expression of life. Make the names of the degrees of vibration familiar so that you may call them when you need their balance, whether it be positive or negative. Perhaps you will find that you are expressing a negative degree of vibration and that you need mental strength. Then lift your spirit high and call the High Priest vibration of Pano Tarot, the Force of Mind, to fuse his Force with your negative vibration, and you will be surprised at how much the new degree of Mind will strengthen you. But take care if you find that you are expressing a positive degree of vibration and never call the High Priest of any of the great primal Forces, for he will bring discord and death to all vibrations which issue the order of positive sex. So also will two negative Forces destroy each other. I beseech you who are seeking to balance your Forces to take care to call the vibration of opposite sex to the one you are expressing, so that harmony may result from the union.

Much has been written on the subject of vibration, which will be helpful to know, and mastering natural law will be of great moment.

The great purpose of my speaking to the people of Earth at this time is that the day for which I have long waited is now dawning, when intuition is developing in the people. And many of them are lifting their spirits and becoming conscious of the world of spirit in which they live, move, and have their being. In this rare state of consciousness, they can comprehend my words and use concentration as directed by the ancient Seers, who knew the law of life. It gives me great pleasure to feel the quickened vibratory movement of Earth and of the people who are responding to the new spiritual understanding which the quickened rate of vibration brings.

Now, I, the Timekeeper, will cease my whispering and speak aloud to the people I have so long guided, that they may know without doubt that light is being given to them which before would have blinded them, and they would have fallen into a state of discord and death greater than that which they already knew.

I, the Timekeeper, have spoken.

Hear the Timekeeper, who has spoken truth.

Sano Tarot.

Concentrate, all you who desire harmony in your lives. Raise your vibratory movement through the balancing of your Forces, to where you can issue the order of master instead of the slave you have heretofore been, and command your Forces to serve you, no longer driven by what you called *circumstance*.

Only those who have raised their vibration to the far reaches of its expansion can enter the royal road of Tarot, which is the higher law of spiritual vibration, and experience the peace which passes understanding.

When the people learn to concentrate their Forces in the balanced way, they will learn the truth of life for themselves. And if my words drive them into action in their seeking for harmony through the raising of their vibrations, the archangels will cry aloud: "Life has triumphed over death, and Earth has been saved from destruction!"

In the King's heart, there is stillness, and each of the Forces which center there moves in its own realm, so there is harmony there. Only in the outer realm of Earth are the Forces separated and mixed until even Hope seems lost among them. But Hope is not lost. It is ever expanding and carrying the people on to perfection. Earth is the great laboratory of life where the seven primal Forces are expanding and fusing themselves under the order of the King, that his kingdom may express on Earth as it expresses in his realm of harmony, where the humming of the seven life Forces makes the music of the spheres.

I, Sano Tarot, who govern the fourth or Inspirational realm of being, have spoken.

Book Three

REPRODUCTION AS THE GODS WOULD HAVE IT

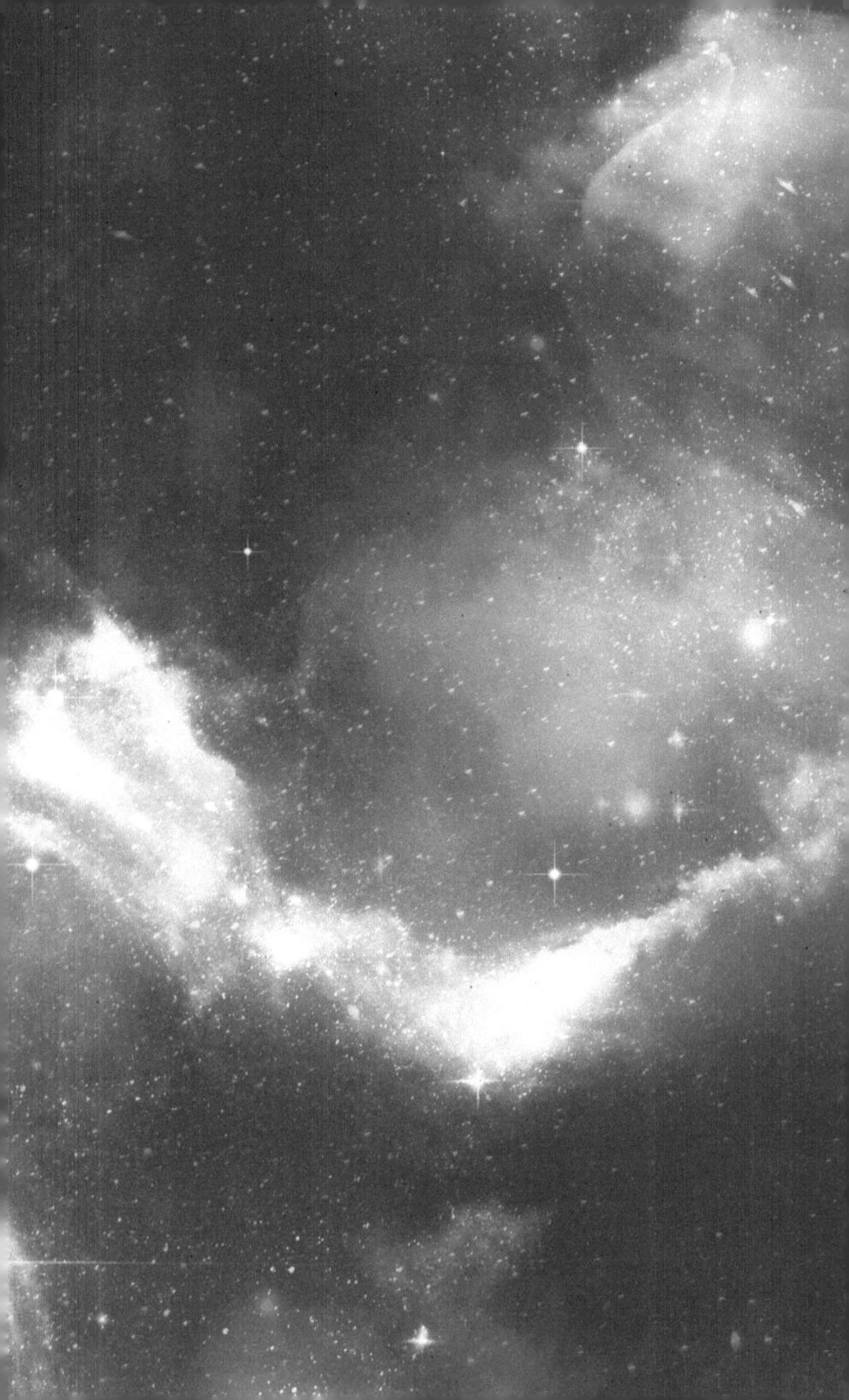

PREFACE

Give close ear to me, my children, who express my Force, Inspiration. You have thought little about the sexual relation as having anything to do with your spiritual development. As a matter of fact, it has all to do with the balancing of the physical and spiritual Forces in the great chemical scheme of life. Because of the lack of the light of spirit, it is rare that the union of their Forces, the people dream of aught but physical lust. So the spirit within them lies with folded wings and cannot lift them into its realm of light and harmony. Sex union is a creative process, and the creations which result from this union take form according to the height of the desire which impels it.

O man, I say to you that woman is the Soul which complements the Fire of your spirit. Approach her with reverence and awe. Within her chalice lies the holy Water, which alone can save you from the Fire which is consuming you. Alas, few men have found her inner court, where springs the alchemical essence which they so blindly seek. Within them is timeless memory, and the spirit of them has not forgotten the beauty and holiness which lies hidden in woman. Awake, O spirit of man, and recognize your savior, Woman!

O woman, I say to you that man is the Fire which complements the Soul, whose symbol is Water, which you contain, and which man seeks in vain because the gods have veiled it even from your own consciousness, until such time as you can bear its light and man can forget the lash of lust and lift his desire to the heights of its spiritual expansion. Then will the veil be rent and you will receive him as your savior. When the spirit of Fire moves over the face of the Water, your creations will be light indeed.

O children of the King, expressing in the dense world of separated Forces, know you this: When harmonious Forces are fused, subtle essences awaken in the bodies of the mates. Essences which man cannot analyze. In them, the music of creation sings. But the mates cannot make them their own unless they lift their desire to the heights on which these essences vibrate. Then the mates become gods indeed and create in the image of the King.

O my people, my heart yearns over you in this dawn of a new day. An understanding of sex, as it expresses in the bodies of men and women, is the most vital need of the people in this dark day which heralds the dawn. I beseech you to develop your channel of intuition that you may see with spiritual vision the signs which are rife. In the day now dawning, gods will walk with men, but only those of you whose physical and spiritual Forces are balanced will be conscious of their presence.

I let my mantle of peace fall over you.

I, Sano Tarot, have spoken.

REPRODUCTION AS THE GODS WOULD HAVE IT

Of all the myriad expressions of life on the planet Earth, there is but one law, the law of sex.

Hear me, Sano Tarot:

I say that of all the myriad expressions of life, sex is the law which governs them. When the people realize this, they will have control of the law of life and thus produce images in the likeness of the King. He has waited long for them to realize the power placed in their hands.

Think, you people of Earth, I beseech you! Only those who think deeply and observe the law of polarity in their unions will see the light of a new day when gods will walk with men, and love and brotherhood will make harmony on Earth.

Think! Learn the god's way of preparing bodies for beings high in their expression of life. These beings are waiting for the people who are awake to prepare, by careful mating, bodies of fine enough material that they may enter them and dwell among the people healing and teaching those of them who give promise of balanced spiritual and physical Forces.

When the people understand the part they play in allowing Forces which have never known harmony to come into their homes, they will think intuitively. And when they think they will raise their vibratory movement, and when their vibration is raised to the height of its expansion, they will never consent to the forming of a physical body whose vibration is low enough to accommodate a thief or a murderer.

Now you are amazed, and it is no wonder, for such a statement is enough to arouse the dormant thought force in all who have ears to hear. And if such has been the result of my words, I am well repaid for my effort to teach you the truth about the vibratory law which governs reproduction.

So you who feel the vibratory movement of amazement, listen again, while you are receptive with wonder. I, Sano Tarot, say to you that those of you who intuitively grasp the truth of the vibratory law of life and readjust your mating according to the law of balanced Forces will be the first to feel the joy which perfect offspring gives.

Hear me, Sano Tarot:

I say that when the people know the joy that perfect offspring gives, there will be none which are imperfect. Bear in mind that sex is universal. Every act is a marriage, and according to the harmony of the Forces fused comes growth or disintegration. Balance your Forces on every plane of expression that your creations may bear the impress of the King. This now will be the burden of my song. When the shadows fall across the land and the long pines whisper together in the wind, I, Sano Tarot, who govern the Force of Inspiration, give ear to the mating songs which call in tones of sweetest music to the parts of themselves which fly in the air on songs of sex, like thistledown with wings.

When the soft humming reaches my hearing, I send a gentle wind to blow the mates together, for should they drift apart, ages may pass before they will be near each other again. I, whose Force of Inspiration is centered in the realm of Venus, sense their seeking and hear the longing in their humming. Then I send Inspiration in the wind and draw them close, and when they fuse their separated Forces, I lean low to hear their cry of joy, for from their union, creation has joined its song to theirs, and the whole universe rings with their mating song.

Harken to my mating song, all you people whose inner hearing can catch the note of truth in its music!

When the song of rising sap throbs through the Earth, I, whose Force is Inspiration, feel its quickening vibration and know that mates are stirring, making ready to give increase to Earth. Ah, it is then that the heart of the universe throbs in unison and the light of creation sends its ray over the land, and I, Sano Tarot, who govern the fourth realm of being, whisper with soft sighing music of love's loneliness without its mate. It is then that I listen for the vibratory note of the mate who is lost in the chaos of unbalanced Forces and only feels that somewhere someone is calling him.

REPRODUCTION AS THE GODS WOULD HAVE IT   89

When in the heart of Nature's mothers a tone of longing hums, I, Sano Tarot, who govern the realm of Inspiration, draw them close to Nature's heart. When the mating season sings of new life, I give ear to the faintest tone which tells of mates approaching. When mates are calling, then music is the sweetest. And wherever there is a feminine Force desiring creation, her vibratory music issues tones replete with longing, and I know that somewhere a blending note is drawing her music to itself and that ere long it will come near, and the longing tones of Nature's mothers will ring out with joyous recognition. And he who draws near will fulfill the law of her being, for when he joins his song to hers, creation will lift its voice and the universe will ring with the music of the spheres.

The balanced channels made by balanced Forces are the hope of the King in that life can express in perfection through them.

Only perfect mates should give bodies to offspring in the realm of Earth, for the vibratory movement of perfect mates is harmonious, and only harmony can express through it.

You see, if only perfect mates created perfect forms composed of balanced Forces, the discordant, unbalanced realm of dense physical matter would not have come into being. Believe me when I say that the people themselves are responsible for the outer, chaotic sphere of Earth and for the imperfect offspring they bear.

Understand that I, who govern the fourth realm of being, and have, through my Force of Inspiration, directed the seeking of the scattered degrees of the primal Forces, know whereof I speak. But, as even I may not interfere with the King's gift of Free Will, I beseech you people, who are waking in astonishing numbers, to use your intuition before seeking a mate, for every balanced mating means a harmonious expression of the life Forces. You see how you may hasten the coming of the peace which passes understanding on the planet Earth, which for so long has known only discord.

Can you think of yourself as a vibratory point in the universe? This is not a simple thing to do. But know you this: You are a nest of vital chemical Forces which vibrate according to their polarization and expansion, and this vibratory movement gives you form and individual expression. There is harmony at the center of your being, else you would not have embarked as an individual entity on the long journey toward the full expansion and fusion of the seven life Forces, for only harmonious Forces can fuse themselves and form the foundation on which is built the temple not made with hands, which is the expression of all the life Forces fused in harmony.

Knowing that you have a center of harmony in your midst should give you hope that the scattered life Forces will ultimately find their balance and make you complete.

Now you who have longed in vain for creation's joyous song, harken to me! I, Sano Tarot, say to you that your desire for balance of Forces has not been strong enough to draw to yourself the Forces needed to reproduce your kind. As you are longing for creation, it must follow that you are expressing your light in a negative manner. Else you would be consciously creating. If you are negative, then realize this, and know that you are drifting through myriads of other vibrations composed of degrees of great primal Forces. These, like you, have been seeking the polarization of their own scattered Force since the planet Earth was formed. In the beginning, the life Forces had reached the limit of their growth and they were separated, that each degree might make its cycle of expansion and become perfect in itself, with knowledge and wisdom gained from contact with all the other Forces. When their cycle of expansion is complete, then the final fusing of the magnetic and electric poles of Earth will sing their perfect mating song, and creation will progress in harmony.

You see how important you are, people of Earth. If one of you fails to grow, the Force which gave you birth cannot become the perfect, full-grown, balanced Force — which is its destiny. You also see the necessity of knowing which Force is yours. You also see the importance of comprehending the law of polarity in the alchemical scheme of life. Knowing which Force is your base gives you illumination as to the law of your expression of life.

Now the question becomes vital as to how to obtain the degrees of Forces which you need to balance, the degrees of Forces which have expanded in your life, through the spiritual will. It is difficult to make you realize the truth of cyclic law. Your judgment lies rather in appearances which you should know are illusions caused by limitation of consciousness. I bid you expand your consciousness and know that the life Forces have entered a new cycle of their expression, during which many things which have been hidden will be revealed. The spiritual will is the opposite of material will, and under its expression, the last shall be first and the first shall be last. "Everything seems to be turning upside down!" is the cry of the people.

Material will moves outward and balances itself with material forms. The *spiritual will* becomes active when the disciple has overcome the flesh and is conscious of a center of balanced Forces within himself. This center sings the song of stillness, and its radiance lights the dark places within him and stirs his dormant Forces into action. Through concentration as directed, these dormant Forces quicken their vibratory movement, and their music sings of the ecstasy of freedom in the realm of creation. Thus through the deep still power of the spiritual will, may the people expand and balance their scattered Forces and know the peace which passes understanding and the joy which belongs to the elect.

We will return to the negative vibration who longs to make creation her song. By way of example, we will say that the great Force of Mind gave her birth and sent her out to grow into a perfect expression of her own Force and then return and add her perfection to her own realm of Mind. But this negative vibration of Mind has not found sufficient polarization of her own Force to give her power of creation.

The subject of sex has ever been misunderstood. Mating has meant only the physical union of the Forces for the purpose of physical reproduction or an attempt to satisfy the hunger of the Forces for complete polarization, which purely physical mating can never give. That their hunger has not been appeased has driven them hither and yon in search for peace, but no peace can express from the union of unbalanced Forces.

When the sex force fell from its spiritual estate, the dense physical world was created, a mongrel, discordant sphere composed of unbalanced Forces.

Children of Earth, I bid you come out of the shadows you have created and lift your desire high, that your creations may bear the impress of the King. It is the order of the King that his rebellious children lift their spirit high in their unions, that his image may be reproduced in the bodies of the mates. When the polarized masculine Forces unite with the polarized feminine Forces, without lust, such power is created that the mates are born again. They are no longer bound by physical limitation. They may ask what they will, and it shall be done, for they are creators indeed.

Know you this: The realm of dense matter in which the Forces have been so long buried is their own creation, and the long journey through the underworld of physical matter is of their own choosing.

When the children of the King let fall their sacred essence, their creations took physical form, and darkness overtook them. This mortal creation has sighed and moaned with no light to guide its weary feet or pierce the veil which hangs over its eyes. In travail, they are born, and in pain, they die — poor, wailing children, born of unbalanced Forces through lust. Only when Love has given of his Fire have they been lifted toward the light. Physical birth and death had no part in the King's plan of creation. The polarization of the life Forces was his law. In the day now dawning, the children of the King will redeem their past mistakes and, guided by the spirit of the King, they will dwell with him in harmony. I say to them that even now, music of harmony sings about them. A song of Love is humming through the dense physical world which they have created. Through their balanced channel of intuition, they may catch its tone and make its music their own. The King is holding out arms of love to lift them to his high realm.

Since many of the people are yet enthralled in the physical world they have created, I say to them that if Love guides their unions, there is hope that they will be lifted toward the light of spirit, where their vision will be clearer, and they will comprehend the primal law of balance.

So there is hope for the negative vibration even though she looks at life darkly through the veil she has woven. Let her think intuitively. What does her persistent yearning mean? At times a voice sings to her of creation, and its tone blends with her longing. But because she knows not her own, she forgets to listen and return the music of its call. She feels that life has withheld its blessing from her. But this is not true. Life has left nothing undone which would awaken her and make her search for strength where strength could be found. She is buried in the grave of matter and knows only that she suffers. The senseless, chattering voices of chaos have hidden the voice of her spirit, which makes high, sweet music within her, the voice of a god which she has buried with her in the tomb she has built, awaiting the release which only she can give through the expanding and balancing of her Forces. So death is claiming her rather than life. How may we help her in her trial? Teach her to concentrate in the balanced way, then bid her feel for herself to which of the great primal Forces she belongs. When she has found her place in the universe, bid her use her own Force in all that she does. When she finds how her spirit soars with the wings of her own Force, she will begin to readjust her life in her new realm of harmony. Now she is less confused and can think, and think she must now, for thought force is generated through the creative power, which the balancing and expansion of the life Forces give.

Bid her think deeply on what a condition of balanced Forces would mean in her life. This realization in itself, will lift her into a higher realm of vibration, for using her thought force must expand her vibratory movement as far as she can think, and meditation will give wings to her thinking. When she knows without doubt that her deep thinking has lifted her consciousness to the height of its expansion, let her request her spirit to make plain to her whether she needs positive or negative Force to bring her nearer the completion of her cycle of expansion.

She who is negative will find that she needs positive balance. Let her meditate on the positive vibrations of the universe. The two positive vibrations which need concern her are the Seers in Higher Vibration and the High Priest of each of the seven Forces. Through deep desire for completion, she may bid them awake and become active in her life. According to the power of her spiritual will, they will quicken their vibratory movement and draw to her the positive degrees of the Forces she needs. She will be conscious of the glowing warmth of new life awakening in her body and will know that the magnetic and electric Forces have expanded within her. When she has found balance through the expanding of her Forces, she will be ready for the final fusion of the balanced Force, which is her opposite. From the union of perfect mates, mortals become gods, and the heavens ring with their mating song.

All you mothers of Nature, overcome your weakness in the god's way, and you will feel the joy of harmonious creation. And the angels will cry aloud with joy, for with every fusion of balanced Forces, the great positive and negative poles of the universe are nearer complete polarization.

All who feel inharmony in their lives may use this spiritual method of expanding and balancing their Forces. Bear in mind that before you have earned this rare privilege, you must have lifted your spirit high and raised your thought force to the very height of its expansion. When you have expanded your Forces and polarized them through harmonious fusion, your spirit will remain in the place where dwells the peace which passes understanding.

The same law applies to all action in the universe. Each Force must express in its own way, and its degrees must be balanced with the degrees of all the primal Forces. When Forces of opposite sex unite in the right realm of being, on the right degrees of their expression, creation takes place, and when the Forces unite in the wrong realm of being on the wrong plane of expression, death and disintegration result from the union.

I sense your request: "Explain again what is meant by the right degrees of expression."

This presentation of basic law is so new and yet so old. However, the people feel its truth and hope surges up through the doubts caused by ignorance and misunderstanding, for alas, too many fail to express harmony in their lives!

When the sexes call each other for the purpose of creation, both mates should feel the call. If such is not true, it may be taken that the mates are expressing the same sex vibration at that time, and only vibrations of opposite sex can fuse themselves in harmony.

One of the difficult truths to present to the people is that both men and women contain both positive and negative Forces, and these Forces are ever-changing in their vibratory action. Thus oft-times, women express positive vibration and men express negative vibration. This, then, is where the utmost care is needed and is what is meant by the right degrees of expression. Should mates both express vibrations of the same nature at the time of union, repulsion will lift its destructive head, and separation and disintegration will begin its deadly work in the bodies of the mates.

I beseech the people to concentrate and think deeply before fusing their Forces on the wrong degrees of expression. Be master of your physical desires and invite Wisdom to sit in your councils. Wait for the mating seasons when the mates express opposite degrees of vibration, that you may know the joy of harmonious creation. Believe me when I say that peace will be your reward.

A new cycle of time is dawning. The spirit of Inspiration is abroad in the land. You may hasten its full expression by observing the law of balance in all your relationships.

It is my privilege to announce that the vibratory movement of Earth has been raised, and the people who are responding to the new swift motion are finding new life, deeper understanding, and wider vision. The chemistry of life is no longer beyond their comprehension. They express the magnetic and electric life Forces balanced through love and are therefore tolerant, compassionate, and wise. I sense your wondering doubt as to this statement, and I assure you that it is true, in spite of chaotic appearances. These are they who, through love, have earned the power and privilege of expanding and balancing the right degrees of all the primal Forces within themselves through the spiritual will. I beseech you to give deep thought to what I have said.

This spiritual union of the Forces may be used to create expressions of art, literature, and music in full perfection of balance and beauty.[8]

My Kingdom of Inspiration issues the order of the Soul of the Universe. The Soul is the mother of life and the body of Spirit. Through the eons, my Force has quivered and sung through my kingdom and the kingdoms of my brothers, inspiring them to the polarization of all the life Forces and so lift themselves back to the realm of harmony from which they elected to fall.

Know you this: The seven kingdoms of the seven sons of the King meet in the realm of Earth and cross themselves, thus fulfilling the order of the King that they absorb each other in harmony, bringing his kingdom into expression on Earth.

My hope is high that the people will comprehend my words. Already my cycle of expression has begun its reign, and in this, my cycle, Inspiration will flow through every balanced form of life.

---

[8] Alas, few dwellers in the realm of Earth know aught of beauty. Beauty has its roots in the lives of those who express it. A selfish man, arrayed in fine garments, well-blended colors and a crown of gold, can give forth no sense of beauty. Art is but mockery when expressed by one who knows nothing of the art of harmonious living. Beauty which appeals to the eye alone can but ensnare the unwary senses of the people who gaze upon it. True beauty is felt rather than gazed upon.

Look back over the history of Art and you will see how little of it has been immortal. Could you look deep into the lives of those great ones who have given beauty to the world, you will find rare souls, even though their daily lives might have seemed otherwise to those who lack understanding.

Beauty is of the Soul, and none can create beauty unless his creation be an expression of the Soul. No matter how the shell is painted or how dazzlingly it be arrayed, it carries only distraction unless from within it sends forth harmony of Forces. True beauty breathes itself out. It cannot be hidden or destroyed and all who contact it find new Inspiration and life.

Bear in mind that beauty is basic, and no surface decoration can deceive the people.

Sano Tarot.

In all realms, on all planes of development, sex union is the law which governs the expansion and action of the life Forces.

The Sano Tarot High Priest is the most powerful vibration in the realm of Inspiration and, when fused in harmony with other degrees of other realms, gives new life and power of creation. But beware, if you are expressing a positive vibration, the High Priest will destroy the degree of Inspiration already yours. In such a case, call the Sano Tarot Seer's Insignia, which is negative, to expand within you.

The vibratory motion of the myriad degrees of the primal Forces gives them color. Imagine the various colors about you — which, you who are sensitive, can sense, even though you may not see them with material vision — of which you are sometimes one and then another, as your own vibratory movement is quickened or slowed according to the harmony or lack of balance in your acts and relationships. In the mass of separated Forces, each degree of colorful Force has its complement, and only when the right colors blend do the complements find each other. The same law makes the music of the spheres, for each vibration hums its own tone and beats its own rhythm as it seeks incessantly for the tone which blends with its own. And somewhere, this tone answers with minor music, for separation makes sadness in its song, and sadness tolls the bell of sorrow for the singing mates who sing alone.

It gives me pleasure most profound to announce that in the balancing process employed by the gods under the order of the King, the singing mates still singing alone in my realm of Inspiration have been drawn close together, and so near is the complete polarization of the positive and negative poles of the great Force, Inspiration, that they await only the final union of themselves to bring this spiritual Force into full expression on Earth.

Now is not this worth striving for, you people who express unbalanced degrees of the primal Forces? Only by raising your vibratory motion can you fuse the spiritual Forces with the physical and so make the balance which issues the order of peace, which you have longed for since the separation, when the Forces were sent out to prove for themselves that polarization is the law.

During the reign of my cycle of Inspiration, what you have called *matter*, which is now in the alchemist's crucible, will be transmuted into spirit.

So in this, the dawn of a new day, once more, I beseech you all to lift your spirit high that your vibratory movement may be quickened. Then you may seek through your spiritual will the Forces you need to make your life complete, and you will find them waiting, poised for their homeward flight.

If my words have made you think, I am satisfied. To those of you who are willing to think, I will say *au revoir*,[9] for truly, we shall meet again.

I, Sano Tarot, have spoken.

---

[9] *Au revoir* (*French*) — goodbye, until we meet again.

Book Four

HERMITAGE SONGS

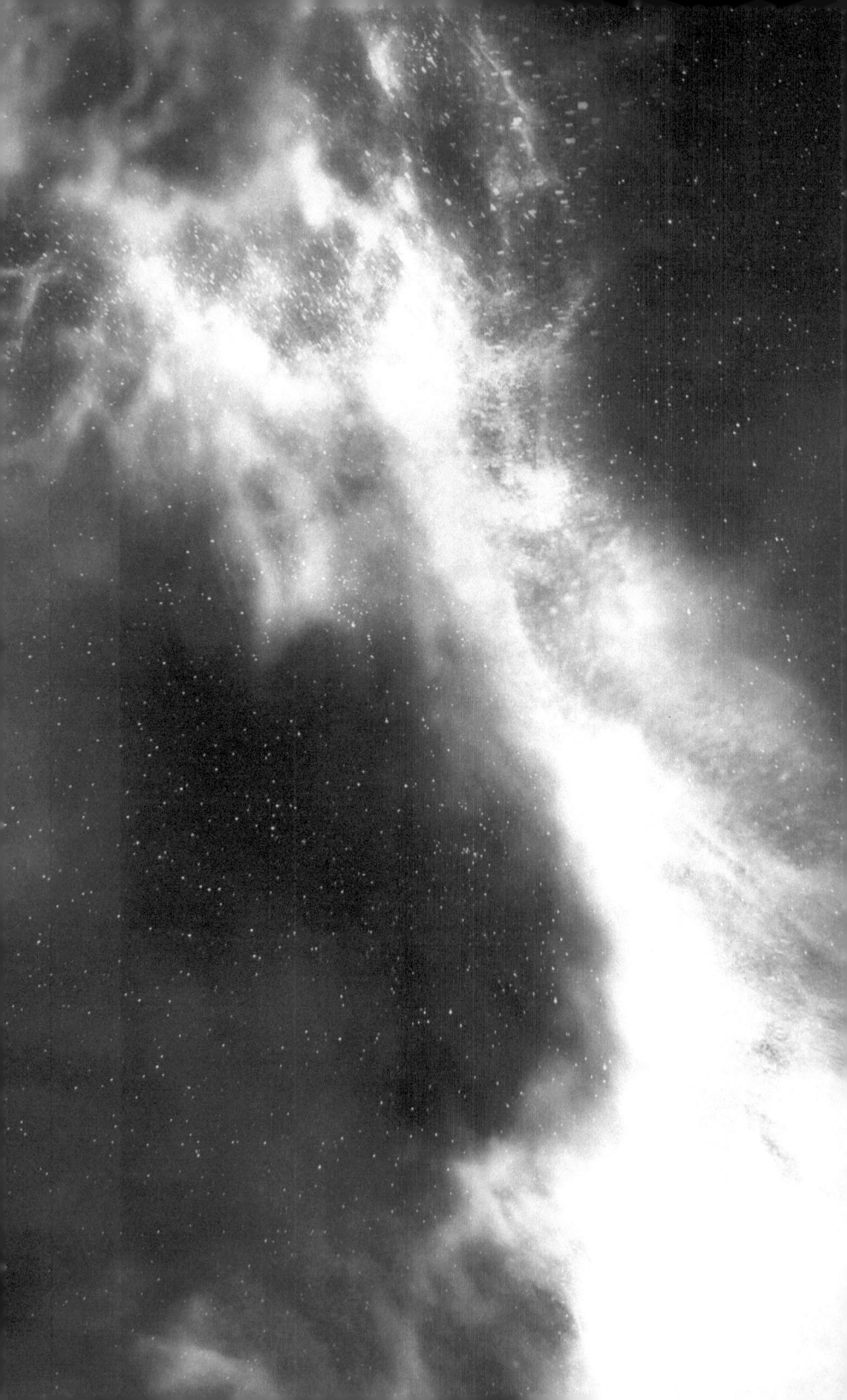

THE SONG OF MOSES

Hear me, Sano Tarot:

Listen deep within you, my people who have ears to hear. The song of Moses makes high music, and not every ear can catch its tones.

The song of Moses was first heard by the angels when the Timekeeper announced that he had succeeded in drawing together a vast number of the scattered degrees of the primal Force, Inspiration.

When this group of expanded degrees of Inspiration coalesced in perfect polarization, a vibratory center of great strength was made in the realm of Soul. This center quivered and sang and served to lead the chaotic Forces in their seeking for balance. Thus in the realm of vibration, Moses came into being.

Harken to the trumpet of the Timekeeper! Long and loud are its blasts. The dead are now waking and taking on the body of spirit. The angels are chanting sweet music, and the tones of their voices swell in perfect accord, for harmony is making the theme of their song, and in all chords of life, it is sounding the rhythm of the spheres.

The cipher Moses signifies the power of leadership. The life Forces expand under cyclic law, and when one of them has completed its cycle of expansion and is ready to begin its reign, bringing itself into full expression, the gods speak the cipher Moses, because all forms of life are being carried forward into a new expression of themselves.

In the echo, the song of Moses now makes mighty music, for the day is at hand when the people will move forward into a new consciousness of life and its law. Old conditions are passing into the maelstrom of worn-out things, and the people need light on the subject of sex, that the ignorance which has caused them so much pain may be dispelled.

Those people who have attained balance of spiritual and physical Forces may be said to be standing on the brow of the hill overlooking the promised land of polarized Forces, where they will find joy supreme.

I beseech them to give ear to Moses, expand their consciousness, and receive the light of the ages, even though the expansion causes a readjustment of their lives. Moses will lead them forward into the peace which passes understanding and the joys which belong to the elect.

Timekeeper, speak to the people. They feel the vibration of your lusty music but do not comprehend its joy.

Most gracious Saint Sano Tarot, I will gladly tell the people the reason for my joy. Through the eons, I have been trying to bring about a condition which would bring harmony to the people I love, and now success is about to crown my efforts. So I am shouting and trumpeting the news, that all who have ears to hear, may know that I, Time, have made ripe the conditions necessary for the final balancing of the great positive and negative poles of life, thus fulfilling the law, which has decreed that the primal Forces shall reunite themselves after they have made seven cycles of expansion in their own realms.

I, the Timekeeper, have labored long in the work of expanding and balancing the scattered degrees of the great primal Forces, that they might be ready when Life calls for their final balancing, and my work gives promise of maturity now. When the King issues the order of balance, I, myself, will bid the angel Gabriel blow the trumpet which has long been heralded, and lo, the realm of Earth will be lifted into a new position, where balance will reign supreme. Thus will the resurrection take place. This, I know, is contrary to the expectancy of the people, but I, who have guided the expansion and polarization of the seven realms of the seven sons of the King, state with positive words that it is true.

The gods have long been satisfied that the ultimate polarization of the life Forces is assured. They know that when the time is ripe, the people will lift themselves into a new vibration, for with the expansion of their own Force, their minds will open, and new light will flow into them, which will show them the way of illumination.

When they see and understand Life's law, they will hasten to live in accord with it, thus resurrecting themselves and fulfilling the prophecy that souls buried in matter shall put on the body of spirit and live anew.

Saint Sano Tarot, will you tell the people of the ancient law, recorded in the beginning, when the King sent the Forces out to expand and develop themselves through contacting each other and absorbing degrees of all the primal Forces and becoming well-rounded expressions of the life Forces expanded seven times?

I, Sano Tarot, say that the ancient law of which the Timekeeper speaks is the same, yesterday, today, and forever. It is the law of balance, and only through the observing of this law can life progress. It has been a long and tedious task which life has set for its goal, that of balancing and fusing the seven life Forces into a perfect sphere.

Before the dense physical world came into being, the seven life Forces expressed the fullness of a cycle of creation. Their positive and negative poles were balanced, and harmony prevailed. This was the period of Eden. The law decreed that the Forces must expand or disintegrate, so it was the plan of creation that these seven balanced Forces fuse their positive and negative elements in such manner that they would each partake of the other and thus expand themselves seven times.

As these vital elemental Forces came together, their combined vibrations created a powerful new force which permeated them as far as its power extended and shattered and scattered them to the four winds. This new force filled them with new life and gave them the power of reproduction. One law was imposed upon these scattered elemental Forces. The primal law of harmony. Give close ear to me, you who are sensitive enough to catch my voice. Make your record clear. I say that the law of harmony was not obeyed by the elemental Forces impregnated with new life and power of creation, and unbalance and discord overtook them.

So great was the power of the newly created force and its destructive reaction when the law of harmony was not regarded in their unions, that it not only scattered the Forces, but drew the whole elemental Force of Material Wealth and the Force of Hope into the vortex. These two Forces, attracting each other, fused themselves under the order of the King and formed a center of balance to which the scattered degrees of the other five Forces have clung in their seeking for balance. The new life received by the Forces has been called *Free Will*. It held them together, and as inharmony in their fusion became their rule, their vibratory movement was lowered until they appeared as a dense mass whirling in space. Thus Earth as the people know it came into being, composed of infinitesimal positive and negative particles of elemental Forces, for although Hope and Material Wealth were not scattered, they expand according to the contact and expansion of the degrees of the other five Forces. They have given freely of themselves and their degrees must be counted as such.

I, who govern the realm of Inspiration, which has served as a spiritual leaven and has lifted the life Forces into a rarer realm of expression, call the high priest Moses to speak to my people and tell them how he has led them out of the wilderness of chaos and brought them to the brow of the hill overlooking the promised land of balanced Forces. Speak, Moses.

I, Moses, will obey the order of the right royal Sano Tarot, by whose order I came into being. With a center of balance in the realm of Soul, the spiritual expression of the life Forces was predestined. The Soul is the body of Spirit and is the mother of life. Creation moves forward in balance and beauty only as the Great Mother expresses the harmony of balanced Forces. The gods, whose work it is to reunite the scattered Forces after balancing them so that they would fuse in harmony with their kind, knew that with a balanced center in the realm of Soul, creation could progress. There was great rejoicing when they knew that after Time had guided them with his wise hand, their perfection was assured. And at the last day of their material expression, a host of them would be ready to be brought together into a harmonious whole, expanded seven times. At such periods I manifest and lead them into a new order of living.

Because through the ages, the Force of Mind and the Force of Heart have balanced themselves with the Force of Material Wealth, Earth has seemed to many an entirely material sphere. But others who have found degrees of Inspiration, Faith, and Love have opened themselves to Hope, and Hope has whispered to them of new growth awaiting them.

In this last day of material maturity, the Force of Inspiration, which has completed its cycle of expansion and is now coming into full expression as the ruling Force of the universe, will rule for a long period of time, transmuting Mind, Heart, and Material Wealth into its own spiritual expression. The vibratory movement of Inspiration is high and swift. It is now sweeping through and lifting into a new state of consciousness, the Forces which have fused themselves in harmony, and the people feel the new spiritual force in great measure.

This powerful expression of the primal Force, Inspiration, surging through Earth and its people, tearing down old traditions and habits of thought, clearing the way for its full expression, is known to the gods by the cipher Moses, for once again the children of the King are being led into the promised land, which issues the order of balance and harmony. The way is not an easy one. The path is full of bare sharp stones which bruise the feet of the wayfarer. The pain of growth is difficult to bear, but I say to you that over the hill is a land flowing with milk and honey. Wide green fields stretch out before you. Deep still waters quench your thirst. O children of the King walking in the shadows, look up and follow me.

I, Moses, have spoken.

THE SONG OF TIMOTHY

By my order, Timothy, who governs the Four Winds of the Inner Court, will speak to you from the Tower of Light, situated in the temple grounds.

I, Sano Tarot, have spoken.

I, Timothy, greet you on this day of grace. Those of you who are sensitive to vibrations of rare nature know that I speak truth when I say that the reign of Sano Tarot has even now begun in the realm of Earth, and others are lifting their vibratory music into higher realms of harmony. Ere long the vast army, which has been likened to the host of heaven, because they express balance of physical and spiritual Forces, will enter the still place of balanced Forces where Love will be their ruler and brotherhood their law.

The Inner Court of the temple of Life is the foundation of the world. Its walls are four square, and there is no flaw in them.

The four walls of the Inner Court are the four basic elements, Fire, Water, Air, and Earth.

My especial work lies in the directing of the vibratory movement of these elements, which make themselves felt in the realm of Earth as the North, South, East, and West Winds. Think of these Winds as vibratory activity and know that all the vibratory activity in the universe expresses in like manner in the body of man, then it will not be difficult for you to relate these great vibrations to the four basic principles of life, Spirit, Soul, Mind, and Body.

Bear in mind that vibration is the law of life. When the gods drew the primal Forces together and held them until they coalesced, these four basic elements were balanced in such manner that thinkers have declared that life is composed of these four elements, and without doubt, these elements are found in all forms of life.

I keep the Four Winds moving at all times. When one of them predominates, it is because there is need of its element in that position, that the polarization of the four elements may be maintained.

Before time was, the element Fire or Spirit, and the element Water or Soul, dwelt together in harmony, they being opposite poles one of the other. They lay quiescent and made music of balance. Then the element Water, which may be likened to a great womb or mother of life, withdrew from her positive pole, the element Fire, and they expanded in their own realms until they had reached the fullness of their expansion. Then under the impulse of creation, the element Water returned to her opposite pole, the element Fire, and from their union was born a cosmic child which the great Mother called *Light* and the people have called *Mind*.

When this creation was mature, a like process took place. Its positive and negative poles separated themselves that they might expand alone. Then the negative pole of Light returned to her mate, and from their union, another child was born, which the Mother called *Form* and the people have called *Earth*.

These four creations constitute the Inner Court of the temple not made with hands and form its four-square foundation. Four gods rule the four basic elements and four angels guard the portals of the Four Winds.

Such profound alchemical knowledge as that of the gods cannot be comprehended by the people, who are shrouded in a material veil of their own making. But the veil grows thinner as their Forces expand, and some of them are catching glimpses of this science.

Think deeply from the center of your being, and much truth will unfold within your consciousness, and light will shine on many seeming mysteries. The gods use these great vibrations in bringing together the right Forces, which must be balanced and fused that life may progress.

When the North Wind blows, light creates new vision in those whom the North Wind touches, and new vision strengthens the spirit. The great element Fire permeates each position where the North Wind blows.

When the South Wind blows, the Soul of Earth is quickened, and new strength of Soul is received by those whom the South

Wind touches. The great element Water permeates each position where the South Wind blows.

When the West Wind blows, Air gives new mental force to all whom the West Wind touches. The great element Air permeates each position where the West Wind blows.

When the East Wind blows, Earth makes men feel its power, for the great element Earth permeates each position where the East Wind blows.

I know it is not easy to comprehend so basic a truth, and you may have to give this mature thought. But the spiritual vision of the people who will carry life forward into a new expression of itself is now more sensitive than ever before, and many will grasp new spiritual truths who but yesterday would have laughed them to scorn.

Elijah, who sings the song of the North Wind, will tell you something of the element Fire as a basic principle of life.

I, Timothy, have spoken.

I, Elijah, greet you in the music of the North Wind. When the North Wind blows, I am pouring spiritual force into all forms of life, and the people breathe into their bodies the White Fire of Spirit.

The element Fire brings purification, and vibrations of rarer nature lift the people when they draw into their bodies the sharp North Wind. Light and heat belong to the North Wind's realm, though this may seem incongruous to the casual observer. Let us examine the properties of the North Wind, and we shall see that I speak truth. First, we know that friction causes heat; also we know that the cold blast of the North Wind causes friction. But what the people may not know is that even though the cells of the body shiver and contract in the North Wind's grasp, if they breathe deeply of it, they will be warmed and not chilled by its touch. The North Wind's reason for being is to stir and quicken the element Fire in every form of life. The North Wind, then, is the element which the gods use to quicken the Fire of Spirit in the bodies of the people. In all forms of life, the element Fire is present. Fire or Spirit is the life-giving element which drives men on to the perfection of themselves. David will now tell you of his element, Water.

I, Elijah, have spoken.

I, David, am the ruler of the element Water. My element is the Soul of Earth and sings in the music of the South Wind. My element is the body of Fire and makes possible the expression of Spirit, which is life. The element Fire alone would consume itself, so the gods used the element Water as a mediator through which Fire could expand. Thus from the mating of Fire and Water, or Spirit and Soul, came moisture which gave the right conditions for both Fire and Water to be of service in the building of a sphere where spiritual expansion is the purpose.

The element Water is the Mother of life, the great womb wherein lay the seeds of creation. Sweet songs of the Soul issue from the element Water.

I, David, have sung to you.

I, Gideon, say to you that the element Air is a vital element. The West Wind carries the music of this element in its movement, for the West Wind is the element Air in motion. Because the people have called the many vibrations of the Four Winds, *Air*, it seems confusing, perhaps, when I say that only the West Wind gives the element Air to Earth and the people. You wonder then how the people live and breathe no air when the West Wind blows not? This now is where I am master, for it is my work to keep the West Wind moving at all times. In the element Air, the Mind dwells, that is, the mental force which gives the power of intellect to the people is composed of the element Air.

Now you see, Spirit had expanded through Soul and could will through Mind, yet it lacked motive for expression. Earth came into being and gave Spirit the force of desire whereby it would seek expansion and development. Zachariah, who rules the element Earth, will tell you about his element, which completes the story of the four basic elements of life.

I, Gideon, have spoken.

My voice is strong and I need no introduction to the people I have long ruled, Gideon.

Well, Zachariah, there is no need that you be impatient. I only wished to link the four basic elements that the people might see how all-important each one is.

True, Gideon, though I doubt not that the people comprehend that without the material side of life, little advancement could have been made by Spirit, for all its expansion and power of will.

Tut-tut, good Zachariah. Proceed with your statement.

Very well, I will explain to the people that which they already know, that materiality plays a most important part in their lives. The people feel the vibration of the element Earth when the East Wind blows. I govern the element Earth which makes possible the expression of Spirit.

Pardon my interruption, I feel impelled to speak out in the echo at this point. I am Timothy speaking. When the North Wind blows the people make progress in spiritual things. When the South Wind blows, the Soul of Earth is stirring, and Spirit expresses in greater measure. The West Wind's blowing quickens the mental force and gives Spirit the power of will, and on the blow of the East Wind, Desire is born, and Desire drives Spirit on to its full expansion. So despair not, children of Earth. Your lives may seem awry, but the true spirit of yourselves is driving on through your various experiences. And when its expansion is assured, you will hear the commendation: "Well done. Enter thou into the joys of thy Lord," which is to say, when Spirit has completed its expansion in the realm of Earth, it becomes master of the law of life, and the people who express its fullness will no longer need the hard trials which lack of knowledge brings. Proceed, Zachariah.

Timothy has spoken.

As you will, Timothy, though perhaps the people would better understand the subject from a more material viewpoint.

Proceed in your own way, good Zachariah, I will not intercept again.

It is well that you do not, Timothy, for without doubt, the people can grasp truth of material nature with greater ease than things of either mental or spiritual nature. This I am sure you will grant me.

I do grant you this, Zachariah. However, the dominant reign of your element is passing, or rather it is being lifted into a higher realm of expression, for you have done your work so well that there will no longer be such need of dense material expression. You must see for yourself that spiritual expansion is making great strides in the lives of many people, and you must hear the vibratory music long heralded as the horn of triumph blown by Gabriel, which means that the long journey of the Soul through your dense realm is nearing its end and the reign of Spirit has begun.

You speak like the hermit you are, Timothy. How can you, who never leave your mountain fastness, observe so much? It is I, who dwell close to the people, who know the vast importance of my element in their lives. Why, then, do you, who at best know mystic lore, presume to dictate to me, who order their lives that they may feel comfort in their daily experiences? Comfort, I tell you, is what the people want, and you say that the reign of my element is passing. Forsooth, man! It is one of your mystic dreams, and my people have no time for mysticism.

Ah, Zachariah, it is ever the old material cry! No time to live, you might as well declare, for mysticism removes the limit of time and makes plain the law of life, which gives comfort to both Mind and Spirit, which is of greater moment than comfort of body alone. So, much as you dislike to acknowledge mysticism, it reaches farther into the lives of the people than mere materiality. Of all the darkness, blind materiality is the most hopeless. What have you to say about this, Zachariah?

Well, I have little to say, Timothy, for it is even more hopeless to give practical knowledge to a mystic hermit. When I have explained my element to the people, they will know that I have argued well and will agree that I am right.

Proceed, Zachariah. Many will agree with you. But others, whom you, yourself, have brought to full growth through your splendid element, will comprehend the signs which are rife and will see with their own eyes that Zachariah himself is changing his methods quite a bit, and they who can read the signs will know that the element Earth is being absorbed in the element Fire.

Well, well, I humor you, Timothy. Now I will place the matter before the people. Listen, you people who have long followed my voice! I say that the element Earth was brought into being that the other three elements of the Inner Court might expand and express. Timothy would have you believe that quiescent mental stuff is greater than my material element, which you can see at a glance, cannot be. For what use would mental stuff be if it could not express itself? And what good would Spirit be, no matter how great its expansion, without power to use its expansion?

My element, Earth, gives form to both Spirit and Mind and creates desire in these forms. So I hold that desire is the greatest gift of the gods to mankind. I know that Timothy would say me nay. But Timothy is a dreamer and cannot be relied upon. Without desire, the world would not have reached its present state of development, for unless a man desires, he will never seek, and if a man seeks not, he will never find that which is his. Now if a man lives his life alone without drawing to himself that which is his, what does his life profit him? Nothing, to be sure.

Also, the element Earth makes the many forms you see. Without this element, there would be no form. So you see, the part the element Earth plays in creation is of greatest importance, though

I grant, Timothy, that Spirit, Soul, and Mind do make great force in my realm. However, I maintain that the people's desires set in motion the elements Mind, Soul, and Spirit. Therefore I object to Timothy's assertion that Earth was made primarily that Spirit might become conscious of itself through expansion.

My element gives great power and beauty, and the things the people can see and prove for themselves are the things which mean more to them than anything else. This is so obvious that any thoughtful person can see its reasonableness. Do not misunderstand me. I have not implied that Spirit, Soul, and Mind are of little importance. But what I do hold is that they are the servants of Earth. There is much to be said on their side, to be sure, and I will admit that I comprehend their arguments better than I once did. However, I am not convinced, nor will I ever be, that the element Earth was created solely that Spirit could expand and express through form. I place my element more positively in the lead every time I sit through their sessions.

I, Zachariah, have spoken.

Zachariah is prejudiced in favor of his Earth element, which is but natural. Did he believe less strongly in his element, he would not have proven so perfect a master, nor would his element have made such strides in its expansion, for so well has he performed his work of perfecting the element Earth that the universe has been given a balance which no other element could have given it.

When the life Forces lost their balance and fell from their high estate into a lowered vibratory movement, chaos overtook them. Before chaos caused them confusion, and inharmony in their fusion lowered their vibratory movement, the element Earth sang a high sweet song and made music of harmony with the other elements. Know you this, that rare song of Earth awaits your singing. Come up out of the chaos of separation and dwell with the gods in the realm of the spiritual Earth.

The chaotic element Earth sang in a shadowy sphere and has been called the *grave* in which the life Forces were buried. It is the alchemist's crucible in the great laboratory of life. Because of its low vibratory movement, it limits the action of the chaotic Forces and saves them from destruction. Limitation causes pain, but through pain, the whole scheme of creation is being refined and ripened, that Earth may lift itself back into the realm from which it fell. This, in turn, will release the Forces enmeshed in its dense body. It is written that a new Earth will rise out of the old chaotic sphere, and the kingdom of harmony will dwell therein.

Zachariah, being the governor of the chaotic realm of Earth, must hold his attention there, so he is quite honest in his argument, but ere long he will plainly see the perfect plan of creation, that Spirit, which is life, has been given three unfoldments, each of equal value. The law of the King decreed that Spirit must descend into a lowered vibratory movement that it might become conscious of itself through desire and will, developed through contact with the many expressions of life. Thus Spirit learns discrimination, and the memory of its former high estate begins to unfold. And with awakened self-consciousness, Spirit lifts itself toward its source, with seven times its expansion when it fell into what has been called *matter*, that it might feel desire and seek experience whereby it would expand.

Thus will the element Earth lift itself into the realm from which it fell when the rebellious children of the King elected to create a dark physical world for their habitation. Now I think you good people understand that Spirit is the essence of life, and its expansion is the prime reason for the expressions of life about you.

I, Timothy, who govern the Four Winds
of the Inner Court, have spoken.

THE SONG OF SAMUEL

Hear the high priest Samuel! He will tell the story of his part in the great balancing process of creation.

Sano Tarot has spoken.

In the beginning, I, Samuel, heard the call of Spirit. I fell into chaos, clothed in fire, scorching my way through the whirling mass of other chemical Forces which had lost their balance when the gods attempted to expand them in harmony. Thus I assisted Uriel in welding together two of the great primal Forces before they were scattered in the chaos of separation. There was great rejoicing when this fusion was completed, for it gave a center of balanced Forces, which steadied the five separated Forces and saved the experiment from failure. In every form of life, this center of balance is maintained and promises the ultimate perfection of the life Forces.

The King knew that the four basic elements, Earth, Air, Fire, and Water, had been successfully fused, and seven powerful elemental Forces of chemical nature had resulted. The King also knew that in the creation of these seven Forces, he had expanded them to the limit of their possibilities, and no further expansion could be expressed by them without the fusion of a new and vital element.

Imagine, if you can, seven vast spheres, each of brilliant color and quivering with a wondrously sweet sound, like the humming of harmonious chords on an organ so great that the whole universe felt its vibration. As your imagination takes hold of my story, observe that while each sphere is separate, yet they penetrate each other until they seem to blend into a color scheme of great beauty. This was the appearance of the harmonious sphere which resulted from the proper fusion of the four basic elements. Here, in this perfected sphere, harmony reigned supreme. Each of the seven Forces functioned in its own sphere, nor sought intercourse with any other than its own.

It was the plan to fuse them all in their right relation as to their positive and negative poles into a perfect sphere. This would have resulted in a sphere expanded seven times through the absorption of each other in harmony.

It would have been simple enough had not the new element given to them brought with it the power of reproduction. Thus was the Garden of Eden destroyed; for like children with a new toy, these vital elemental Forces lost all sense of harmony and fused themselves with elements not in harmony with them. This caused discord. The King showed them their mistake and besought them not to misuse the power he had bestowed upon them, that they might expand in harmony. But the will of freedom, so newly given them, caused them madness, and they would not heed the order of the King.

Then the King drove them out to learn for themselves, through bitter experience, that harmony is the law and that without it, no good thing can be. You have heard this story before, but I am sure you cannot hear it too often, for it strikes at the very base of life. When the primal Forces ran wild with their new freedom and power and fused themselves promiscuously, thus hurling themselves out of the realm of harmony, they separated into myriads of infinitesimal particles, each a spark from one of the primal Forces. Each spark which had fused itself with a particle of one of the other Forces without regard to the law of polarization was therefore feeling pain and discord in its center. As lust and promiscuity became their rule, their vibratory movement was lowered until they appeared as dense material forms.

To be sure, in all that whirling discord, there were some particles of the Forces which remained true to their own element and fused themselves in harmony with the law, which has decreed that only elements of like nature and the right balance of positive and negative expression can expand in harmony. The sparks which drew harmonious elements to themselves in the beginning have been the hope of the gods, for they knew that if one particle of the scattered Forces could find even a degree of harmony in all the discord about it, that ultimately, after they had proven that harmony is the only law which will give them health and happiness, they will reunite themselves under that law, and the will of the King will be fulfilled. Thus was perfection predestined from the beginning. I will request Uriel to tell you something of his work. I will speak to you again, but what I have to say will be more easily comprehended and visualized after he has given light on his part in the scheme of creation. Speak, Uriel, I pray you.

I, Uriel, say to you that I work in the realm of White Fire, which the gods call *cohesion* and the people call *love*. When the harmonious degrees of the primal Forces draw close enough to each other to feel attraction, I hold them together until their fusion takes place, and I rejoice that with each fusion of harmonious Forces, the whole universe balances itself in like measure.

Let me say that love which holds its mate in bondage must not be confused with the Force of Universal Love, which knows no selfish purpose and gives freely of itself for the service of Life. This will require deep thought on the part of the people. Profound thinking will raise the vibratory movement of the thinker, thus making the task of the gods more simple, for the understanding of those who have power of thought will become clearer, and the basic law of life will be quite plain to them when they have raised their vibration to the height of its expansion.

You know that attraction draws together and holds harmonious Forces. You also know that it has been the work of the gods through the eons to balance the scattered degrees of harmonious Forces and that this will result in the reign of harmony, which has long been heralded. My work of cohesion is more simple now, in this, the dawn of the reign of Sano Tarot. Would that you all had knowledge of the chemistry of the gods that you might more fully comprehend the scheme of life's expansion.

I, Uriel, have spoken.

Peter will now go on with the story of the Forces as expressed in the bodies of the people.

Sano Tarot has spoken.

It is my pleasure to speak, Saint Sano Tarot. I will tell the people something that will bring the truth of the seven primal Forces very close to them, and they will no longer think of them as unseen, vibrating currents of air. No. The Forces which are expanding and balancing themselves on Earth are the people. When a given number of degrees of the Forces have coalesced, they form a center of vital, intelligent Forces, strong enough to take form as an individual entity. These forms are like unto the Forces they express, and during their period of Earth life, by harmonious fusion with other degrees of Forces, their vibratory movement is quickened, and they expand and are filled with new life. The chemistry of life is indeed profound.

I, Peter, have spoken.

I, Samuel, say to you, good people, that through diligent delving, profound intuitive thought, and knowledge of the law of polarization, Peter discovered that this law is the law of vibratory expansion. Thus it has been said that Peter holds the key of the temple not made with hands which endureth forever. You see, Peter thought deeply and honestly, even denying what he could not comprehend, but always seeking the light. Then the promise that he who seeks shall find was fulfilled, and Peter knew the truth hidden in age-old parables and symbols, all of which tell the same story of the primal Forces which lost their balance through the misuse of Free Will and fell into chaos, that through experience they might become conscious of the law of polarization, whereby growth and expansion might be theirs.

Polarization only could have saved the primal Forces from the long journey of pain which discord always brings. But harmony was not thought of by the mad Forces. They fused themselves promiscuously and wondered at the pain in their lives.

When sickness and death overcame the Forces, the cry went forth that death must come to all and could not be avoided. Now death had no place in the perfect scheme of creation, but is the result of the inharmony in the fusion of the Forces in the bodies of the people. Had they been content to observe the law of polarization in their unions, their expansion would have been natural and within the law, and the dire pain and death suffered by them because of discord in their mating, would have been unnecessary.

In this, the beginning of a new cycle of expression of the Forces, whose vibratory movement is of rarer, swifter nature than the dense material cycle through which they have just passed, the scattered Force of Inspiration has been successfully drawn together. And now, after ages of learning, through bitter experience, that harmony is the law of growth, the knowledge of the people who express this spiritual Force will become like that of the gods, and their need of travail on all planes of expression is even now growing less.

When the rebellious Forces lost their balance and fell into the chaos of separation, the King knew that an ideal must be given to them so that they would not lose hope of ultimately finding peace. So, I, Samuel, volunteered to join the light of Spirit to the darkness of their material chaos by beckoning them on toward new experiences which would further prove to them their mistaken use of Free Will and drive them forward in their expansion of consciousness. I have never ceased my efforts, and I have seen many souls awaken to an understanding of the law of harmony after long ages of blindness and pain.

Many of them have felt my presence when the way was dark. My hope is that they will be eager to hear more, and what is of greater importance, that they will heed the teaching of the gods and make harmony the law of their lives.

I, Samuel, have spoken.

I, Sano Tarot, say that Samuel has spoken truth.

THE SONG OF JUDITH

Hear me, Sano Tarot:
  I bid you give close ear to Judith of Israel's forces in the Sun. Speak Judith.

I, Judith, will speak of things profound. I will endeavor to make my story as simple as possible, that your minds may not be confused by terms of alchemy. I beg that you will bear with the many repetitions in this document. It is a truly scientific process which will result in the expanding of dormant brain cells, thus rending the curtain of limitation which hangs before the altar room of your temple. The day is at hand when the temple veil will be torn asunder, and a vast host of people will comprehend the truth of creation in terms of natural law.

Seven Forces constitute the whole of life in the universe. Everything is made by the fusing of degrees of these Forces, so believe me when I say there is nothing else.

You see so many things which seem to differ so widely that this statement is difficult to accept. However, when you understand that the life Forces were scattered into infinitesimal degrees of themselves, and that each degree shows itself as a separate expression of life, my statement seems more rational, and should a degree or particle of these Forces expand through joining to itself another degree of a harmonious Force, it changes its form, sometimes an almost imperceptible bit, according to the strength of the new degree fused with it. Then again, such new life is taken on by the expanding Forces that the change in their expression is evident to all.

You see, while the forms may be different and called by different names, yet in essence, they are the same, for each is made of like material, their difference in appearance being the result of the fusion of different degrees of the life Forces. This now is the puzzle of life laid before you. It is the plan of creation to expand these degrees of the scattered Forces to the full measure of their possibilities, then to further perfect them by fusing with them another degree of Force which harmonizes with them until they express all the primal Forces balanced in harmony.

Let us take seven fluids, each a-quiver with life, and each of a given color. We will place them in separate vessels, but the master chemist knows that these fluids can be fused in such manner that each would partake of the other, making a combination of perfection and beauty. He also knows that ere he can accomplish this, he must fuse a new element with the seven fluids, which would cause them to absorb each other and so expand sevenfold. In the scheme of creation, this element was called *Free Will*.

Those of you who have followed the teaching of the gods in the Hermitage recognize this story of the fluids as the same story of the Forces developing in the realm of Earth.

Moreover, they recognize in it the perfect plan of the gods, who have been directing the fusion of the Forces throughout the eons.

Sano Tarot has spoken.

As an illustration, we will say that the seven primal fluids were poured together, each remaining true to itself, refusing to mix one with the other. The chemists, most truly, had a delicate task to perform, for the new element, Free Will, which must be given them to bring about their absorption, could cause expansion to such extent that separation, rather than fusion, would result. Now this was what occurred. The fluids became separated into myriads of drops of themselves, each quivering with the powerful new force given to them by the solution, Free Will. This gave them the power of attraction and reproduction, and they gathered together or fell apart according to the harmony they found in their selection, for all of these quivering drops were not in harmony with each other.

As discord filled them, their vibratory movement was lowered and slowed until they seemed to stand out as dense entities, complete in themselves. They set up a kingdom of their own and elected Free Will as their ruler. In their chaotic state, they forgot the law of the King, which is harmony, and Free Will became license and led them hither and yon into further separation and pain. The creations resulting from their inharmonious unions became more dense and discordant, and thus the dense physical world came into being.

The gods watched their mad whirling from their dwelling place in the King's heart and volunteered to leave their high estate and dwell in the midst of chaos with the Forces, limiting the action of Free Will until such time as they could bring the Forces back under the law of harmony and so keep them from destroying themselves.

Instead of despairing, the master chemists of the King's domain knew that in time, by carefully fusing the harmonious drops of the seven separated fluids, he would attain the same result, in that the fluids would be brought to the full measure of their solution, having absorbed each other in harmony and expanding seven times, making the same marvel of perfection he had first dreamed of.

If you use your intuition deeply, it will be simple to comprehend the plan of the universe. It does not require much meditation to realize that the seven primal Forces — Mind, Heart, Material Wealth, Inspiration, Faith, Universal Love, and Hope — are very real Forces in the lives of the people. Neither is it difficult to understand that these seven virtues, developed to their full possibilities, would make a perfect man or woman.

The method of fusing the separated degrees of the seven primal Forces expressing in material bodies has been little understood by the people, who, because of the lack of spiritual vision, which unbalanced Forces give, could not know that the fusing of their Forces is a vibratory and spiritual process which results in either imbalanced creations of lust, or spiritual expansion and regeneration, according to the desire and motive which impels the fusion. The fusion of the life Forces is accomplished through the polarity of the sex relation on all planes of expression.

Hear me, Sano Tarot:
Physical marriage is an effort of the gods to bring together and hold harmonious Forces, in that there is then hope of harmonious

creation. I beseech the people to think deeply on what I have said and observe the law of harmony in their unions that they may know the joy which the creations of balanced Forces gives. Proceed, Judith.

I, Sano Tarot, have spoken.

In this matter of the fusion of the spiritual and physical life Forces, I will speak as plainly as possible without the use of alchemical terms, for when a new idea is presented to the mind, it is not easy to grasp in its fullness, although, I assure you, that this idea herein presented to you is as old as our good recorder, Time. New ideas bring new brain cells into action, and these cells must develop by continued use before they can hold a well-rounded idea and drive it into action. So it will take time and concentration before all the people grasp the truth of this basic law. Much is purposely left unsaid in this document in order that the people may use their intuition, through which illumination will guide them aright.

When the people think deeply before taking their marriage vows and are sure that their Forces are polarized, great expansion of consciousness will be theirs, and their creations will express beauty and harmony. When physical offspring is desired, let them regard this law of vibration and fuse their Forces only when attraction is strong within them both. Should either mate feel repulsion, a child of inharmony will be the result, and separation will enter their own lives. In such cases, many feel that their love has grown cold and that they are drifting apart. The cause of the trouble is that they have broken the law of their polarity and brought inharmony into their relationship. No fusion of Forces, where there is even a degree of inharmony, can cause anything but disintegration and death.

During the long ages I have dwelt in the Sun, I have assisted the gods in their work of transmutation. Transmutation is their way of building the many forms in which the Forces are expressing, and my good people, there is but one way to transmute, and that is by fusing an element with one already vital with life's essence. Great care must be taken that these Forces are harmonious, else they will destroy rather than transmute themselves into something greater than they were.

Kindly allow me to speak a word here. I am the hermit, Israel. I am deeply interested in Judith's story for it strikes at the very heart of life. I caught Judith's voice in the echo and have called my brothers to harken to its sweetness and truth. I rejoice that the miracle of sound, transmitted to Earth from the Sun, has taken place. I could not refrain from speaking out in the echo when I felt the miracle occurring in the ether. Speak on, Judith. You have given me profound pleasure.

I greet you, father, and rejoice at your call.

Yertoh!
    I, Sano Tarot, say that this cipher means that an event long hoped for has taken place and great joy is felt in the Hermitage.

Imagine a vast sphere of separated particles of primal Forces. Like a whirling sphere of stardust, it looked when the gods began, by delicate handling, to select and fuse the tiny particles which were in harmony and of opposite poles of magnetic and electric force. Should they attempt to fuse two particles of an element, both of which were negative, repulsion would result, and should they attempt to fuse two positive and negative particles of antagonistic elements, destruction would result. So you see, the gods have had no simple task in making the realm of Earth as the people know it today.
    From seven atoms harmoniously fused, man began his development in the realm of Earth.
The Timekeeper has spoken.

The Timekeeper has given you the truth of predestination. When the gods succeeded in drawing together and fusing in harmony atoms of the seven primal Forces, they knew that after ages of infinite patience, all the scattered Forces would find their balance, each partaking of the other, so that instead of being a sphere of partial perfection, expressing degrees of unbalanced Forces, Earth would evolve from chaos into individual expression of all the life Forces in perfect polarization, thus proclaiming that predestination has been fulfilled.

The many degrees of the scattered Forces which have not found balance are spoken of as the lost. However, nothing is lost in the great alchemical scheme of creation, and these unbalanced degrees of primal Forces may find balance in great measure by observing the law of polarization in their marriage relation.

This is the Law. Fuse only harmonious Forces and let the fusion take place only at the mating seasons. That is when attraction is felt strongly by both mates. At such time it may be taken that the harmonious Forces are expressing opposite poles of vibration, one of the mates being positive and one of them negative. Then, and only then, through the polarization of harmonious Forces, will new life and growth enter the expression of their lives.

Bear in mind that when Forces are fused when repulsion or antagonism exists, the law of polarity is broken and their creation is born in travail, and disintegration and death fall over the Earth. Judith, proceed.

Sano Tarot has spoken.

I, Judith, invite your attention while I tell you of the original plan of creation, which is the same, yesterday, today, and forever. I call the children of the King to return to their Father's house and live under his Law which they broke when they fell into chaos through the misuse of Free Will. It is the Law that the sexes unite, but the prime reason for this union is the balancing of the physical and spiritual Forces in the bodies of the mates. This is the divine creative process. Through the combined desire and will of the mates for perfect polarization of their Forces, these Forces are lifted to higher planes of vibration, and the result of their fusion is the birth of spiritual power and physical regeneration.

It will be difficult to make the people who have lived so long under the lash of physical sex hunger understand, but it is true that physical generation had no part in the original scheme of creation. It was the plan that the children of the King fuse their Forces and, through polarization and absorption, maintain their high estate as creators of themselves, made in the image of the King. Physical birth or death had no part in the scheme. These calamities came into being when the sex force was inverted and became physical lust. The feminine side of the Forces was the first to feel physical sensation, and she whispered of her discovery to her mate, and he followed her leading. Thus their vibratory movement was lowered and the dense material world came into being, and gods became mortal, with only a submerged memory to remind them of their high estate.

Give close ear to Judith, who speaks truth.

Sano Tarot.

Because she caused the downfall of the life Forces, I say to woman that the regeneration of these Forces is her responsibility. I bid her lift her desire out of the realm of sensation and emotion and give back to her mate, his godhood. Thus, through self-control and knowledge, she will become the woman clothed with Spirit; with generation mastered, she will redeem her mate, and together they will be gods indeed.

Only the few will grasp the truth of my words. To the great mass who yet dwell in the throes of generation, I say: "Develop your balanced channel of intuition and move in the light of its guidance."

Saint Sano Tarot, I have told the people who have attained sufficient balance of Forces to quicken their power of intuition, all that is necessary at this time, without going into realms which they cannot comprehend. I have not told them of the time which is now at hand when the scattered Forces have balanced themselves in many of them to such extent that they are now powerful magnetic and electric centers, expressing in radiant forms, worthy of their high estate. With your permission, I will request Samuel, who has played so great a part in their spiritual expansion, to tell them of the gift of the gods to the elect.

Your request is most graciously granted, Judith. Speak, Samuel, I pray you.

Sano Tarot.

It is with pleasure that I speak of the supreme gift of the gods to the elect. The elect are those who began their harmonious fusion when they were as stardust in their separation and have observed the law of harmony throughout the eons since the primal Forces were scattered and driven out to learn that without harmonious balance, there can be no growth. This lesson has been learned through pain and discord. Now a vast host of people have attained a balance of Forces which issues the order of Light in the realm of Spirit. They express as radiant centers of Light, and their radiance is easily discerned by those who contact them. These are the people whom the gods call the elect, because of the balanced movement of their vibratory expression; they have been elected to steady and inspire the less balanced and, therefore, weaker people, who, because of their lack of harmonious fusion, have disintegrated rather than welded their Forces.

These people who have attained such magnetic and electric balance of Forces have power to draw to themselves the Forces still separated from their cycle of balance through their spiritual will, which is the will of the King and gives freedom indeed.

This will make physical marriage unnecessary for these children of the King, in the polarization of the Forces whose combination makes them what they are. When the day of balanced Forces issues its order throughout the realm of Earth, there will be no more physical childbearing, neither will there be sickness or death, for these are caused by the imbalanced condition of the life Forces. Then the gods will walk with men and the peace which passes understanding will envelop the Earth.

I sense many questions regarding this statement. To you all, I say: The key to the temple is harmonious mating, and you may find your complement on all planes of expression through balanced concentration or developed intuition. This is enough of such profound truths at this time.

I, Samuel, have spoken.

I, Judith, say that the high priest Samuel has spoken well. You see, Samuel is ever present in the realm of spiritual expansion. He stirs the latent Spirit within the people, and Spirit is the essence of life. He has kept the fire of Spirit burning, knowing always that in the process of expansion, Spirit, which is life, would expand until all the life Forces had been transmuted into its high realm. At this time, man cannot conceive pure Spirit as Samuel knows it. In the time of which he speaks, the radiant beings who have lifted themselves from mortal man to spiritual man will dwell with the King in the realm of Universal Love. This realm is not in some far-off place but is here in your midst, awaiting your recognition of it.

In the beginning, Samuel volunteered to leave the realm of Love and enter the dark realm of material Earth as the torchbearer and remain in its midst until every living thing had felt the fire of Spirit kindle within it, for Samuel knows that when once the people feel the drive of Spirit, nothing can stop their seeking for light until they find it.

The day of which Samuel speaks, when there will be no more physical childbearing or sickness or death, as compared with the eons which have passed since the polarizing process of universe-building began, is not so far away. Already here and there, light is dawning in minds awaking from the sleep of material coma, and gods are peering from once dull eyes.

Remember that millions of like periods have passed since the gods began the seemingly impossible task of expanding and fusing the myriads of particles of the seven life Forces, and you can readily see that to them, the day is at hand when the prophecy that Fire, which is Spirit, will ultimately consume the Earth, will be fulfilled. This is not a fearful time to anticipate, for when the seven primal Forces — expanded to their full measure and balanced in harmony in the realm of Earth — Universal Love will dwell with men, and all things material will have been transmuted into Spirit. Spirit descended into the grave of matter that it might feel desire and thus be driven toward the fusion of itself with the other elements and save the whole scheme from destruction.

You who have balance of spiritual and physical Forces and can sense the perfection of this day when Spirit will reign on Earth, know that the elect will dwell here in harmony. You are wondering why no new bodies will come into manifestation at this time. You must know now that the reason for the existence of Earth as you know it, is that the Forces might expand and fuse themselves until they express balance and thereby fulfill the law. Earth is the fusion ground in the laboratory of the gods.

When the law has been fulfilled, there will be no further need of physical fusion of the Forces, so no new bodies will be formed. The gods will then form a new planet, composed of the same Forces which are still far from polarization, just as the planet Earth was formed, only its beginning will express balance in greater measure than that of the beginning of the planet Earth.

You are wondering what relation the planet Earth will have to the new planet formed for the expansion and development of the Forces, which have lagged in their polarization because of mating without thought. This is a question most profound, for the regenerated Earth will be the only planet in the Sun system where the seven primal Forces have attained balance. You comprehend that the seven planets or realms of being, each express one great elemental Force, and life, which you see expressing in so many forms in the realm of Earth, had its beginning in these centers of Force.

Seven rays of light, breaking into prismatic colors in a lowered vibratory movement, each color seeking its complement that it might be made whole again.

Joseph has spoken.

Truly spoken, Joseph. Earth is the balancing sphere where the careful fusion of these prismatic colors is taking place. And when perfect balance has been attained, the new realm formed by the yet unbalanced Forces will swing quite close to the regenerated Earth, which will act as a sun or magnet of balance to the unbalanced sphere and thus hasten its harmonious expansion.

Now you are asking if the seven planets are inhabited? Yes. All Force takes form, but this form is not varied as when fused with other elements. So but one form of life expresses in each of these realms, according to the nature of its essence. Only in the realm of Earth do these Forces fuse themselves.

The planet Uranus dances and flashes like the pure spiritual Fire it is, and its form is like that of flame.

The planet Neptune takes form like unto a mountain of luminous nature.

The planet Venus takes form like an oval gem of radiant beauty.

The planet Mars swings like a giant red Earth in the ether.

The planet Jupiter takes form like unto a heart.

The planet Mercury is like a keen-edged weapon.

The planet Saturn is like a seed quivering with life.

I am using symbols to express the nature of the Forces, which have their centers in these luminous bodies. By the positive action of the Sun on their negative poles, they center their given Forces in the planet Earth where their polarization takes place.

A chemist can better comprehend the scheme of expansion and development employed by the gods in fusing these Forces in harmony in a lowered vibration. Polarization is the perfection toward which they have patiently worked since the beginning of the creation of Earth.

Now I am going out of the echo. I am standing on the temple steps, and I raise my right hand to you.

Peace be with you.

I, Judith, have spoken.

Judith has retired into the altar room. She will come again into the echo at another season.

I let my mantle of peace fall over you.

I, Sano Tarot, have spoken.

THE SONG OF ISRAEL

Hear me, Sano Tarot:
I bid you harken, singers of harmony! Life's liberty bell is pealing out the message of the ages. Let the ears which are attuned to the music of the spheres hear the high, sweet notes of freedom lifting themselves in the ether. No longer are the children of men driven hither and yon in blind seeking for peace. Now they are clothed with strength. The grave cloth has fallen from their eyes, and they see with vision clear the divine plan of the ages.

Here in the Hermitage dwell the mystic brothers whose very existence has been called a myth. Little has been written about us, and that little has been false, owing to the limited vision of the author, who, mayhap, did dream of mystic hermits, else caught a glimpse of truth from ancient lore or divined the hidden meaning in age-old symbols. Thus a few thinkers have delved deep in the mysteries.

Give close ear to silence, all you people who sing the harmony song, and you will hear the sweet accord of Gano Tarot's music. While pulsing through these mellow tones, Love runs clear and sweet, and every life which reaches up toward higher things adds its tone of beauty to Life's great orchestra, and trembling birds give light and grace to it. Deeps profound are touched by the master Wisdom. Speak, Israel.

I, Sano Tarot, have spoken.

I, Israel, say that discordant notes from the lower realms quickly bring guidance from the teachers nearest them. But alas, the people who know not harmony are blind and deaf to wisdom's words. And oft-times, those who would help them must needs leave them alone to become balanced through life's experiences to such extent that they turn of themselves toward the light of the ages for guidance.

Ah, it is then that in the Hermitage, the elder brothers of the great family of humanity sing praises, for when the people seek wisdom, new songs of Hope join their notes to the harmony song of the universe, which has its center here in the Hermitage.

You have learned that harmony is the keynote of polarity. Where harmony is not, the life Forces disintegrate and scatter. Now that you comprehend the law of life, let us take counsel together, that the wisdom of the ages become plain to us, and the following of the perfect plan of building the temple not made with hands will be as simple as building a house of blocks, first made perfect by the artisan's hands.

Let us play at temple-building. It is a game most profound and requires thought and intuition, for in the making of the pillars which uphold the temple spires, material must be gathered from the four corners of Earth and molded into perfect forms of perfectly balanced colors, each fitting in its own perfect niche, with no flaw anywhere. Think not that the material will be easily found or that ages will not pass ere it be gathered together. The gods began to play this game in the beginning of the creation of Earth and are now beginning to see the near completion of many pillars which are lifting themselves straight and strong beneath the dome of the temple of life.

Long ages ago, when the gods knew that the pillars were taking form and color and that, ultimately, all the stones would be laid in their places, they held a council and laid the cornerstone of the temple not made with hands. The cornerstone of the temple not made with hands is harmony, and the people are the pillars standing on the cornerstone, which is its foundation.

Listen when the moonlight lays over the cornerstone, and you will hear sweet humming and feel still peace within you, for the moon sings of receptivity, and that which is received in harmony makes Hope lift its voice. And when Hope sings the harmony song, Life leans close to listen, for then creation has fitted a living stone in the walls of the temple not made with hands.

Israel has spoken.

I, Sano Tarot, say that the hermit Israel has spoken truth. Israel, request the high priest Solomon to come into the Tower of Light and tell the people of the part he has played in the building of the temple not made with hands.

I gladly do your bidding, Saint Sano Tarot. I command you, slave Sirus, to go and bid Solomon come into the Tower and speak to the people.

Good master, I, slave Sirus, go.

Hear me, Sano Tarot:
I say that the slaves of those who dwell on the heights of spiritual expansion are elemental forces which have not begun their expression in material form. These forces cannot reason, but they can do the bidding of a strong mental impulse and can carry vital messages and do vital deeds when driven by vital force. At this stage of their development, they grow only by reflected will. This they blindly sense and are held by powerful centers of force, that they may be filled with life and driven into action. The gods use these elemental forces in many ways, thus advancing them in their development. We will now give ear to Solomon, who will tell you more about the temple not made with hands. Solomon's part in its building has given to it its name, and even to this day, men gather in temples of stone in memory of Solomon, though few of these modern neophytes dream of aught but the letter of Solomon's law. In ancient days Solomon dreamed only of building the spiritual temple through material means. Greetings, Solomon. Speak, I pray you.

Greetings, Saint Sano Tarot and the people who have ears to hear! Situated in the sacred heart of every man is the cornerstone of the temple not made with hands. Long have I labored to fit it there in such perfection that they would feel its guidance and see with clear vision the orderly plan of the universe, whose keynote is harmony.

In the beginning, when the seven primal Forces separated into infinitesimal particles of themselves, I listened patiently, knowing that when they began to feel their separation, loneliness would overtake them, and they would seek surcease from its pangs. When I detected in all that discordant vibratory humming, a minor tone, I listened for another tone which harmonized with it. Then I directed the Four Winds to blow them this way and that, always drifting them toward each other until they were close enough to feel attraction. Then they no longer needed my guidance, for they came straight without a turning to each other, and when they sang their song of love and new growth possessed them, creation gave to the temple of Life a new and perfect stone.

Then Life matured this perfect stone, and in the night watches when all was still, I listened to the soft minor whirr which told of the awakening of the spirit of this creation of Love. Then from afar, by the action of Life's law, which is vibration, another minor note sings softly.

Ah, how my love songs have rung out through the ages and how all-absorbing my work has been!

Love is the great cohesive force which cements the stones in the wall of the temple not made with hands, and when Love finds itself alone, it seeks for balance in the laboratory of life, and when harmony sounds the keynote of Love's seeking, I, Solomon, who am the master builder, give direction to it. When the lovers whose keynote is harmony meet in the moonlight of receptivity, again creation builds its perfect stone and fits it into its perfect place, where it awaits Life's maturing. So from the beginning has the temple been built.

When lovers have mistaken lust for love, then have my eyes been wet with tears, for they have torn asunder Life's most precious gift, and what might have hastened the completion of the temple has been destroyed.

I, Solomon, have spoken.

I, Sano Tarot, say that the high priest Solomon has spoken truth. Life is the temple dome, and the polarized degrees of the scattered primal Forces are the perfect stones which fit in their places in the temple building. Think intuitively on this record of primal law, and you will never allow inharmony of spirit to draw you into marriage. This is the unpardonable sin, and all through the ages, you will suffer and die for thus breaking the law of your being.

We who have guided the harmonious fusion of the life Forces see the lights which the balancing of the magnetic and electric life Forces gives. And we liken them to the host of the elect, which means that a vast number of people have observed the law of harmony throughout the ages and have balanced their cycle of material Forces and are now ready to move forward into the new cycle of Inspiration which is gaining in momentum with each new day. You, my people, see their material bodies and call them well-balanced men and women.

I call them the elect. Israel calls them the harmony people. Solomon calls them the pillars which uphold the spires of the temple not made with hands. Moses calls them the leaders of the chosen few who will enter the promised land — chosen, not because of favor but because they have earned their high estate. Samuel calls them children of Light. Timothy calls them children of ancient heritage because they began their polarization when they were as stardust in their separation.

In the beginning, the tiny particles of the separated Forces were indeed fortunate when, in all that whirling chaos, they found themselves near a particle of Force which harmonized with them and, through their fusion with it, gained a degree of balance which served them well, as it gave them strength, thus enabling them to draw more readily other particles needed for their expansion and growth.

My Force, Inspiration, expresses the realm of Soul and flows through its symbol, Water. Since the beginning, wise gods have directed the element Water through the planet Earth, for well they knew that without moisture, material forms would wither and die. Moisture comes from the mating of Fire and Water. The element Fire is the Spirit of the planet and Water is the Soul. My Force of Soul has long been absorbed in Spirit, which comes through the Sun, and what has been absorbed in the planetary development has also been absorbed in the bodies of the people, for all of life sings together in the balancing of its Forces.

It is because of the completion of the polarization of Spirit and Soul that the Earth feels new life and the thought of my people is being lifted into higher realms, and the reign of brotherhood is dawning. Out of the material night, a new day is dawning. This Soul Force, which issues my order, is making itself felt in all forms of life, and without attempting analysis, my people are changing their habits of thinking and living. Many of them are finding that less material food is required for the nourishment of their bodies.

Believe me when I say that the old order of living is passing into the maelstrom of worn-out material and will join the laggards on the path toward illumination.

Ah, my people, give time to the teaching of spiritual law. Think intuitively and lift your vibration to the height of its expansion. Then you will see that I have given to you the truth of the ages and the law of the prophets.

Take harmony as your life song and let its tones lift themselves above all others in your every thought and act. Thus you will hasten your expansion of consciousness and be among those who are beloved of the gods and who are now standing on the brow of the hill overlooking the promised land. The promised land is the reign of harmony on Earth, now in its inception. The archangels are crying aloud, and Gabriel has blown a mighty blast on the trumpet of the Timekeeper. And at the sound of its note, the minds of the people are opening like flowers which lift their faces to the Sun, and lo, the pure Fire of Spirit is burning its way through the old density of material thought, and new light is sweeping through my people in all their expressions of life.

Issue the order to yourselves that you give rein to your spirit and let it fly in the sunlight of truth. Then I, who govern the new cycle of Inspiration now making itself manifest, will reach out arms of love and keep you from falling by the way. When once your spirit soars to the height of its expansion, it will draw your mind and your heart, and your body with it. Then peace will settle like a dove upon you, for you will have found the still place where the King speaks and Love rules.

Verily, I, Sano Tarot, say this, which is truth.

THE SONG OF THE KING'S HARPIST

Lift your spirit high, my people, and give close ear to the music of the King's harpist.

I, Sano Tarot, have spoken.

My harp is attuned to the high sweet tones of love. And it is a privilege to strike a chord of harmony here in the Sun and feel its vibrant notes quiver through you and out in words so crystal clear that souls just waking from the sleep of material coma can sense their beauty, for brotherhood is the theme of their music.

When the people whose songs are of discord and sorrow long to sing of harmony and joy, listen in their heart of hearts, new tones will be heard, like the humming of strange, sweet music, with peace in its alluring notes, and Life will lift their spirit to where the sunlight of truth makes clear music in the orchestra of the spheres. When truth and clear vision sing together, Life opens the temple gates, and lo, wide green fields and deep still waters stretch out before them. While they rest within the temple gates, there comes to them the sweet piping of the King's messenger, which lures them forward toward the temple door.

Ah, it is then that the gods rejoice and the angels chant sweet music, for when the pilgrim on life's journey stands before the portal of the temple, there is little danger that he will fall by the way, for the giant Strength has placed his power within him and fear has no longer a hold on him.

Far agone are the days when the Earth whirred and hummed in discordant tones. Order has appeared in the chaos of separated Forces. Only in the outer world of illusion does confusion still sing. My harp has never ceased its music deep in the heart of the universe. Beauty has trembled in its notes, but until the Timekeeper bade me strike a stronger chord, few had done more than sense its melody. Now, a great and powerful choir is lifting its chords of harmony in such music that all through the universe, hearts which are attuned to life's higher songs are vibrant with quick response, and lo, they sing a song whose rhythm is love and whose keynote is brotherhood.

I, Sano Tarot, say that it is indeed a time for rejoicing, for the noise of falling towers and the dust they bring can no longer deafen and confuse those whose vision sings of knowledge and understanding.

All you good people who will read my words, listen in the still watches for the tones of a new song, whose volume increases with swiftness unbelievable, even to those accustomed to rapid changes. Know you this: The song you hear is the song of brotherhood. Let its music fill you each and every one, for it will lift your spirit into realms of harmony where you will find the peace which passes understanding.

Service is the note of the cycle now dawning, and love is heard like the ringing of a golden bell through its expression. Where no love sings, service is but noise, and its blatant tones scream in the ether making discordant music on the planet Earth.

Those who seek to bring about the age of brotherhood for self-exploitation had better by far tie a millstone about their necks and leap into the sea, for without doubt, Love trembles when the name, brotherhood, is spoken. And Love is a jealous master and destroys the renegade who trifles with his sacred essence.

Brotherhood will express in the realm of Earth only in such measure as Love has first quickened the hearts of the people. Love comes only to those who have learned to serve with no thought of self. And it is my good pleasure to acquaint you with the fact that there is a vast host of my people who have attained the high plane of selfless service. And I have been assured by the gods who have guided them when they have called that they are of sufficient numbers to carry humanity forward into the realm of spiritual expression where harmony will prevail, and brotherhood will be the law.

I, Sano Tarot, who govern this realm of Soul which is sweeping the elect into a new order of living, issue the order that my people lift their spirit high and give free play to joy, for lo, the reign of

Spirit sings of victory over the reign of materiality which has held Earth in its thrall.

My breath sends out whisperings of joy. The ecstasy well-nigh causes my breathing to cease. Pardon my interruption. I am Ruth, who loved much.

Ruth speaks well, for joy has reached great heights here in the Hermitage. The King's harpist will resume his singing.
Sano Tarot has spoken.

Good people of Earth, my music rings like sweet-toned bells high in the ether, and waves of light roll upward from the realm of Earth with the sound of whirling winds, which blend their sweeping notes with Life's great orchestra.

Light hums its way through the universe like the notes of many orioles, and those whose ears are attuned to its music may lift their voices and blend their songs with it. When the people sing of Light, understanding gives rarer quality to their song, and when the chords of understanding fill their song, tones of wisdom give depth to its beauty. It is then that the throbs of love fill Light's song, and when Light sings of understanding, wisdom, and love, the great overtone of brotherhood creates a new song in the music of the spheres.

Children of Earth, the new song of brotherhood awaits your learning. This song is my theme. Would that you could behold the city of brotherhood already prepared in the ether about you. Be still and listen to its song. When your inner ear catches its high music, Life will bid Light sing to you of understanding, wisdom, and love. Then in the twinkling of an eye, your own song will blend its notes with the song of brotherhood, and you will hear the order to go forward into the promised land where joy supreme awaits you.

I, the King's harpist, have sung to you.

THE SONG OF THE MAGICIAN

Hail, children of the King! Clothe yourselves with garments of light that you may stand out clearly in this the dawn of a new day. Out of the dark, you come walking toward the light. Stand on the white wool of a lamb and show the pentacle, which it is your right to wear. Bear no false witness as to your place in the temple. The King is not mocked. Your seal is plainly visible in the white light of Michael, lord of the Sun.

Tie your mantle with a golden cord. Place your hands on the altar and give yourselves to the service of mankind.

Give us a sign, has been the cry of the people from the beginning. This is the right demand, for unless the people desire to know, they are but sluggish cells, and life does not deal gently with sluggish cells.

No greater sign can be given them than that they behold a balanced life and see with their own eyes regeneration at work, rebuilding and transmuting a dense material body into the pure gold of spirit.

My position in the Hermitage is that of the magician. Bear in mind that the true magician proves his power but uses it only that good may be for the whole. Materiality is of great importance, for Earth is holy ground, but the true magician is not held by it. He is magician indeed who can laugh at poverty and pain. To such, life gives freely of its richest blessings, and lo, a paradox is here! The true magician also laughs at his blessings. Nothing can hold him as he moves along his path. Neither good nor evil influence him. He knows that life is moving forward toward the perfection, which is its goal, and that no act of his can change the great scheme toward which creation is trending. His will is merged with the will of the King, and no shadow can fall across the path of him who dwells in the light of understanding.

True magic is the science of the gods, and the people who lift their spirit high and comprehend the law of life, which is harmony, may know that words spoken by them bring quick results. It is true indeed that the people give account of their spoken words, for spoken words set vibrations in motion which carry their power far, as a pebble thrown in still water sends its movement to the farthest shore. Words are bodies of forces, which once set in motion, move on through endless time, building or destroying, according to the will which sent them forth. Moving spiral-wise, they return in due season and cross the lives of their creators. Set a watch at the door of your lips, children of the King, that the fruit of your words be blessings. Search your motives and purge them of selfish desires. When you desire blessings for yourself, desire them also for your less fortunate brothers, that your desires may purify themselves.

No magic is greater than the deep desire of a selfless man.

Give deep thought before the performance of a ritual. Know that vibration moves out in circular form from your own center. Its power is determined by your balance of Forces.

What swings high also swings low. It is in the vast radius of a vibration created through ritual that danger, as well as construction, lies.

Once there was a being of great power, who, by his will, created a vibration which should have guided the Forces in their destiny, but alas, when his creation touched the lowest point of its cycle, he was filled with the force he had created and lifted his hands high and spoke the words: "I have all power! Worship me!"

Then the force of his creation dragged him from his high estate and enmeshed him in the net of his material will, and even though he had been ordained to stand as the light of the world, yet he hurled himself into chaos and the expansion of the life Forces was delayed through him. Legend has called him Lucifer.

I beseech you never to perform a ritual until your lives have been purged and the light of Spirit fills your being. When you raise your arms and call powerful forces into action by your will, I say to you that they take form according to the harmony of your subconscious realm, where lies the memory of all time. Where harmony is not, no good thing can be. This discourse I am giving to you because I desire that you think deeply of the inner side of ritualistic practice. It is based on profound knowledge of imaging, dominated by will. Move slowly with outer practice of rituals.

Today, in this the beginning of a spiritual dispensation, I say to you that there is but one key to illumination and that key is fashioned by your character and by the acts you perform in your daily lives.

Many have been ordained to assist the gods in ways not obvious at this time, but I say to you that the maturity of your constructive ideals lies entirely with yourselves. Lucifer, the hope of the gods, fell into chaos.

The vibratory movement of the planet Earth is quickening with swiftness unbelievable. Be not afraid to live. Within you lies the full solution of your life. I beseech you to lift yourselves in mind and body that all who contact you will be filled with peace and courage. Center your Forces. Be master of your life. See that your foundation has no flaw in it and that its four corners are square and perfect. Keep your eyes on the ark of the covenant situated in the center of your body.

Chaos is about to fall over the Earth. And those of the people whose foundation is rotten — the golden cement which once held the stones together having melted in the fiery furnace of unbalanced Forces — are losing themselves and will be compelled to begin their long journey toward the Sun of Spirit all over again, their foundation being only the original immortal spark, which they have so neglected.

Hold fast to harmony that your lamps may be burning with a clean flame when you are called into service. O children of the King, you are very dear to the gods in the Hermitage. Your names are known and your motives are closely observed and recorded on the Timekeeper's record.

Be steadfast in faith. Give freedom to all, that you yourself may be free. Time moves swiftly now. Flow as a sparkling stream with the great river of Inspiration, knowing that the course of the river is under the guidance of the gods and will reach its goal in due season.

Harmonious groups who work together in full agreement on one purpose generate magic power, and their purpose shall be fulfilled. Bear in mind that harmony is of chemical nature and does not mean that the personal lives of the people must be in full agreement. Each member of a group through which spiritual magic can express must bring a quality or element which will give balance to the elements of all. Thus we have a combination of Forces balanced in harmony, which has naught to do with personality. When such combinations of Forces have fulfilled their purpose, they separate and fly apart, seeking new affinities for other purposes. Draw close, children of the King, that the gods may have your allegiance in the construction of a new and better world.

I, the Hermitage Magician, have spoken.

I, Sano Tarot, say that the magician has spoken truth.
I let my mantle of peace fall over you.

THE SONG OF MICHAEL

I, Michael, lord of the Sun, declare that the hour has struck! O people of Earth, I bid you know that the Fire of Spirit is burning white under the alchemist's crucible in which you dwell. The dross you have drawn about you is being burned away, leaving you naked before the throne.

I am the all-revealing Light which flows out from the heart of the King. All things are revealed in my radiance. The deep unsuspected motives hidden in the hearts of the people who dwell in the shadows stand like demons on the King's highway. Search your motives, children of Earth, and wash the stains from the tablet of your lives while there is yet time. Lift your spirit high and follow its guiding voice.

Mighty movements are sweeping through the realm of Earth. Age-old towers are falling with deafening noise. Tremble all you people whose material veil has not been rent. Verily I say to you that the time of harvest is upon you. You must reap what you have sown. Woe be unto those who hide behind the veil of illusion, in this the day of the burning of the tares.

Hear me, Sano Tarot:

In the realm of living, my people, who express the great primal Force, Inspiration, will lead all others in this my cycle of expression. The day is at hand when living conditions will undergo drastic changes. No longer will one demand service from another. When my cycle, now dawning, increases its motion in the realm of Earth, it will be the law that each individual earns the space he occupies in the universe.

Give thought to the changing world, for I say to you that chaos is about to fall upon you. Those of my people who have found the still place of Spirit will be lifted above the confusion of reconstruction, but I beseech you to believe me when I say that those who have willfully lagged in their expansion will wail in the darkness which ignorance makes its own.

Hear them cry, good Father! Even now, their wailing trembles in the ether.

Light has spoken.

Would that they might enter the Tower of Light and see with understanding the wisdom of the ages. Little children, think, I beseech you! When you think intuitively, you raise the vibratory movement of your body, and when your body is lifted into higher realms, life and its complexities will be of simpler nature, and lo, the perfect plan of creation will lay before you like an open book.

It is my good pleasure to say to you that from the Hermitage, where the gods dwell, the new motion of the dark planet Earth is plainly visible. The dense material mist about its form has become of rarer nature, which means that the material Forces are yielding to the transmuting power of Michael's Light, and great rejoicing is lifting the songs of the Seers on the height of spiritual expansion. The sweet humming of new tones is heard rising from Earth.

O my little ones, whom I have kept close in my heart since the beginning, when the rebellious children of the King elected to build a dense material world for their habitation, lift your spirit high and rejoice with those who have watched your pain and progress since you appeared as bits of sacred Fire whirling like stardust in the midst of chaos.

The Timekeeper has ordered the trumpeter to blow a blast of triumph, for the prophecy that the dead shall rise from the grave of matter and put on the body of the Spirit is about to be fulfilled.

I bid you who have the power of thought to lift your consciousness and feel the new vibration about you. Come up on the heights, and let us sing together of love and immortality. Here is the peace which passes understanding. I hold my hand high to you!

I, Sano Tarot, have spoken.

I, Michael, lord of the Sun, say to you that I am clearing the way for the children of Light. My force of transmutation is sounding the death knell of all that is untrue and is stirring the very bowels of Earth.

I, who know no quarter, am sweeping through the governments of Earth, tearing down their false traditions and revealing their selfish hearts. Woe be unto those who govern the people for selfish gain. My Fire is scorching away their cloaks of hypocrisy, leaving them writhing and blind, for those who cannot bear the light of Spirit are blinded thereby.

I will scatter their gold which they have hidden away, that their weaker brothers may not know hunger and want. My flaming sword will cut them from their moorings, and they shall know no peace.

I, Michael, have spoken.

Hear me, Sano Tarot:

I say that Michael speaks truth! The cycle of balanced Forces has begun, and in all spheres of life, balance will express. But before balance can express much purging must be done. Michael, whose flaming sword destroys, also builds swiftly when the way is cleared. Many are the doomed who will fall in the lake of bitter waters during the great purging process. But know you this: Life will lift them into new realms of endeavor in due season. My Force, Inspiration, will sing in loud tones through and above the wailing songs of the people. Children of Earth, lift your spirit high and give close ear to my song, that you may join your song to mine.

When the day now dawning has reached the sunrise, the glory of the King will shine about my people. I call you, my own, into service!

I am singing! Note the changing forms of life's expression. I am sweeping through them with ever-increasing measure. Children of Earth, be prepared to stand right royally on the rock of harmony, for on this foundation, darkness will not enfold you in the days of chaos which are even now coming to pass. Know you this: Out of chaos will come light and understanding, such as has never before expressed on Earth.

Ah, my land of ancient Egypt! I see you rising out of the dust of the ages and lifting your radiant heart once more to the sun of spirit.

I flow like a mighty river. Many are they who will leap out of the river and languish on its banks. But the river flows on with ever-increasing power and purity. Lift your spirit, children of Earth, and flow with me. I let my mantle of peace fall over you.

I, Sano Tarot, have spoken.

I, Michael, lord of the Sun, wrap my mantle of light about the dark planet Earth.

THANK YOU FOR READING!

If you enjoyed this book, please consider leaving a review, even if it is only a line or two. It would make all the difference and would be very much appreciated.

Sign up for our newsletter to be the first to know when new books are published and receive a free bonus:

radiantbooks.co/bonus

OTHER TITLES PUBLISHED BY RADIANT BOOKS

THE LAND OF THE GODS
by H. P. Blavatsky

Hidden in plain sight for 135 years, Blavatsky's story is a beautifully written account of an exceptional journey into Shambhala. Immersive and engaging, this profound book will provide you with a unique outlook on the deeper side of life, exposing our true nature, interior powers, and ultimate destiny. It explains grand, spiritual ideas more thoroughly and swiftly than any book you'll ever read.

THE BOOK OF THE GOLDEN PRECEPTS
by H. P. Blavatsky

Full of incomparable beauty and inspirational power, this book reveals the Secret Path to Enlightenment followed by the greatest spiritual teachers of all time, such as Jesus Christ and Gautama Buddha. If you're seeking real spiritual growth, if you long to access divine wisdom that will explain everything that is happening in the world, if you want to live with deeper and majestic purpose, this book is your key.

REVEALING COSMIC MYSTERIES
by H. P. Blavatsky

Lost for over a century, the full stenographic reports of meetings with Blavatsky in London have resurfaced recently. Immerse yourself in those very meetings at which Blavatsky revealed secret knowledge. The questions others posed may well have been your own, and her answers will unlock your deeper understanding of the Universe's profound secrets. You will be privy to Blavatsky's inspirational power, brilliant and penetrating mind, sharp wit and authentic wisdom.

THE DIVINE GOVERNMENT
by Helena Roerich

A secret for many years, this book provides the first-ever evidence showing how the Divine Government, known as *Shambhala*, helped the United States during the Franklin D. Roosevelt presidency. It outlines profound principles for becoming a true leader who can guide any nation to prosperity by building just relations between the people and the state.

THE TEMPLE OF MYSTERIES
by Francia La Due

Bridging spirituality and science, this classic work is a true gem of the world's esoteric legacy. The Master Hilarion, the Protector of America and Europe, transmitted it through Francia La Due, intending to assist humanity in resolving the challenges of modern civilization and guide us toward unity with the cosmic forces that shape our existence. *The Temple of Mysteries* will illuminate your path to self-realization and help you find answers to the most pressing questions that trouble your soul.

FROM THE MOUNTAINTOP
by Francia La Due

Uplifting and poetic, this book invites you to rediscover your true essence and forge a future illuminated by the light of resonant wisdom. It is a collection of high vibrational messages of truth and beauty that imbue the very aura of humanity. Transcending time and space, these messages radiate the healing energies of faith, hope, and love. For those who aspire to embark on the Path toward Mystery, *From the Mountaintop* will serve as a celestial beacon in troubled times.

OTHER TITLES PUBLISHED BY RADIANT BOOKS

THE MYSTERY OF CHRIST
by Thales of Argos

Eye-opening and heart-touching, *The Mystery of Christ* brings a fresh perspective, an uncommon insight, and spiritual depth to the dramatic events which occurred two thousand years ago. As you read the profoundly stirring pages of this beautifully crafted narrative, you will comprehend the unequalled mission of Christ and the innermost secrets of Mary, culminating in an unexpected encounter with the new mystery of the Cosmos named Sophia.

THE LIVING WATERS OF JOY
by Grace Lucia Kimball

Through heartfelt revelations, this book will become your sanctuary — a spiritual oasis where your troubled soul can always find comfort, peace, and renewal, even in the most difficult of times. Like a healing balm, its eloquent prose flows as a gentle stream of living water, offering you a profound and uplifting experience of the Higher Presence.

BECOMING WHAT YOU ARE
by Two Workers

Drawing on timeless spiritual wisdom, this book will take you on a journey toward self-realization and inner awakening. Its inspiring messages and practical advice will show you how to cultivate the qualities necessary for spiritual growth. It will help you align your actions with your highest potential and ultimately become what you are — a radiant and awakened being.

OTHER TITLES PUBLISHED BY RADIANT BOOKS

THE SEVEN LAWS OF SPIRITUAL PURITY
by Two Workers

Providing a profound and eye-opening perspective on achieving true spiritual purity, this thought-provoking and straightforward book draws practical advice from ancient wisdom to show you how to purify your mind, body, and soul. It is a passionate plea for a better world — a world in which humanity no longer has to accept and deal with the consequences of many sufferings but instead prevents their very causes.

THE KINGDOM OF WHITE WATERS
by V.G.

For a thousand years, this secret story could be told only on the deathbed, for it revealed an inaccessible garden paradise hidden in the Himalayas — Shambhala, a place thousands of people searched for, but always failed to find. Each carrier of this secret story took a vow of silence that could be broken under only two conditions: when facing imminent death or in response to another's persistent requests for knowledge about the mythical Kingdom of White Waters.

www.ingramcontent.com/pod-product-compliance
Lightning Source LLC
Chambersburg PA
CBHW060608080526
44585CB00013B/728